Malcolm X and Black Pride

Lucent Library of Black History

Anne Wallace Sharp

LUCENT BOOKS
A part of Gale, Cengage Learning

Detroit • New York • San Francisco • New Haven, Conn • Waterville, Maine • London

LIBRARY OF CONGRESS CATALOGING-IN-PUBLICATION DATA

Sharp, Anne Wallace.
Malcolm X and black pride / by Anne Wallace Sharp.
  p. cm. -- (Lucent library of black history)
Includes bibliographical references and index.
ISBN 978-1-4205-0123-0 (hardcover)
1. X, Malcolm, 1925–1965. 2. African American Muslims--Biography. 3. African Americans--Race identity. 4. Race awareness--United States. 5. Afrocentrism. I. Title.
BP223.Z8S57 2010
320.54'6092--dc22
[B]
                                                           2009038463

Lucent Books
27500 Drake Rd.
Farmington Hills, MI 48331

ISBN-13: 978-1-4205-0123-0
ISBN-10: 1-4205-0123-2

Printed in the United States of America
1 2 3 4 5 6 7 13 12 11 10 09

Printed by Bang Printing, Brainerd, MN, 1st Ptg., 01/2010

Contents

Foreword   4

Introduction
The Evolution of Malcolm X   6

Chapter One
A World of Violence and Segregation   10

Chapter Two
"Detroit Red"   24

Chapter Three
Minister Malcolm X   39

Chapter Four
A New Name—a New Outlook   57

Chapter Five
The Death and Legacy of Malcolm X   75

Notes   93
For More Information   97
Index   99
Picture Credits   103
About the Author   104

Foreword

It has been more than 500 years since Africans were first brought to the New World in shackles, and over 140 years since slavery was formally abolished in the United States. Over 50 years have passed since the fallacy of "separate but equal" was obliterated in the American courts, and some 40 years since the watershed Civil Rights Act of 1965 guaranteed the rights and liberties of all Americans, especially those of color. Over time, these changes have become celebrated landmarks in American history. In the twenty-first century, African American men and women are politicians, judges, diplomats, professors, deans, doctors, artists, athletes, business owners, and home owners. For many, the scars of the past have melted away in the opportunities that have been found in contemporary society. Observers such as Peter N. Kirsanow, who sits on the U.S. Commission of Civil Rights, point to these accomplishments and conclude, "The growing black middle class may be viewed as proof that most of the civil rights battles have been won."

In spite of these legal victories, however, prejudice and inequality have persisted in American society. In 2003, African Americans comprised just 12 percent of the nation's population, yet accounted for 44 percent of its prison inmates and 24 percent of its poor. Racially motivated hate crimes continue to appear on the pages of major newspapers in many American cities. Furthermore, many African Americans still experience either overt or muted racism in their daily lives. A 1996 study undertaken by Professor Nancy Krieger of the Harvard School of Public Health, for example, found that 80 percent of the African American participants reported having experienced racial discrimination in one or more settings, including at work or school, applying for housing and medical care, from the police or in the courts, and on the street or in a public setting.

It is for these reasons that many believe the struggle for racial equality and justice is far from over. These episodes of discrimination threaten to shatter the illusion that America has completely overcome its racist past, causing many black Americans to become increasingly frustrated and confused. Scholar and writer Ellis Cose has described this splintered state in the following way: "I have done everything I was supposed to do. I have stayed out of trouble with the law, gone to the right schools, and worked myself nearly to death. What more do they want? Why in God's name won't they accept me as a full human being?" For Cose and others, the struggle for equality and justice has yet to be fully achieved.

In many subtle yet important ways the traumatic experiences of slavery and segregation continue to inform the way race is discussed and experienced in the twenty-first century. Indeed, it is possible that America will always grapple with the fallout from its distressing past. Ulric Haynes, dean of the Hofstra University School of Business has said, "Perhaps race will always matter, given the historical circumstances under which we came to this country." But studying this past and understanding how it contributes to present-day dialogues about race and history in America is a critical component of contemporary education. To this end, the Lucent Library of Black History offers a thorough look at the experiences that have shaped the black community and the American people as a whole. Annotated bibliographies provide readers with ideas for further research, while fully documented primary and secondary source quotations enhance the text. Each book in the series explores a different episode of black history; together they provide students with a wealth of information as well as launching points for further study and discussion.

Introduction

The Evolution of Malcolm X

Malcolm Little, better known as Malcolm X, overcame a tragic childhood, a teenage period of rebellion and crime, and seven years in prison to become one of the best known and most controversial African American voices during the 1950s and 1960s. Journalist Charles Whitaker elaborates: "He was born Malcolm Little . . . but the world came to know him as Malcolm X, a provocative spokesman for black nationalism whose words inflamed the passions of thousands of Black Americans struggling to wrest free from the disabling grip of poverty and racism. . . . [He] became a figure of almost mythic proportions."[1]

Malcolm grew up in the Lansing, Michigan, area, where he and his family were victims of the prejudice, discrimination, and violence that characterized African American lives in both the North and the South during the 1920s and 1930s. His childhood was both traumatic and tragic, as journalist Desair E. Brown explains:

> Nothing but trauma and tragedy seemed to meet the family with their settlement in Lansing, and it hit them head on. Between the burning of the family's home, the brutal murder of Mr. Little (a murder that went unanswered and unsolved), the commitment of his mother to a mental in-

stitution, and his bounce from foster home to foster home, life in Lansing was a downward spiral.[2]

Malcolm X's teenage years were spent in Boston and New York City, a time during which the young man turned to drugs, alcohol, and crime as a way of life. He was arrested for committing a burglary and sentenced to ten years in prison. It was while he was imprisoned that Malcolm underwent a transformation. He began to read voraciously and also converted to the Islamic faith as practiced by the Nation of Islam, an African American religious organization that believed that blacks were not only the original race of people but the superior one.

Upon his release from prison, Malcolm Little took the name Malcolm X, symbolizing the unknown last name of his African ancestors, and became one of the Nation of Islam's most powerful ministers. He was devoted to the Nation's leader, Elijah Muhammad, a charismatic preacher who became a father figure to the young Malcolm. Once proclaiming himself the angriest black man in America, Malcolm X spoke out against the evils of racism and discrimination. In urging other blacks to use any means necessary, including violence, to obtain equality, he was often referred to by the white community as a hatemonger and revolutionary. Author Alex Haley says: "No man in our time aroused fear and hatred in the white man as did Malcolm because in him the white man sensed an implacable foe who could not be had for any price—a man unreservedly committed to the cause of liberating the black man in American society."[3]

After a break with the Nation of Islam and a pilgrimage to the Islamic holy city of Mecca, Malcolm underwent another change. Prior to his pilgrimage, Malcolm had been a severe critic of the civil rights movement's call for integration. He had more than once expressed a belief that the nonviolent practices of Martin Luther King Jr. were not the best method of achieving equality. Following his pilgrimage, Malcolm began to consider the possibility of cooperating with the civil rights movement in an effort to speed up the movement toward black freedom.

Any chance of such cooperation ended with Malcolm's assassination in 1965; he was not yet forty years old. Despite his early death, Malcolm's message of black self-sufficiency and freedom

Malcolm X was known for his powerful speaking skills.

has persisted, and his legacy lives on in the hearts of other black activists who continue today to call for complete equality for black Americans.

Historian Peter Goldman elaborates on Malcolm's life and priorities: "He thought of himself as a teacher, a minister, a Muslim, an African, an internationalist and, in the most general terms, a revolutionary; and before any of these things, as a black."[4] Malcolm himself perhaps summarized his life best: "I am not a racist. I am against every form of racism and segregation, every form of discrimination. I believe in human beings, and that all human beings should be respected as such, regardless of their color."[5]

Chapter One

A World of Violence and Segregation

Malcolm Little was born on May 19, 1925, in Omaha, Nebraska. His father, Earl, was a Baptist preacher from Georgia; his mother, Louise, was Earl's second wife. She was a light-skinned, well-educated black woman from Grenada in the British West Indies, who got her light-colored skin as a result of the rape of one of her ancestors by a white man.

Malcolm was the fourth of eight children born to Earl and Louise Little. He also had three half siblings from his father's first marriage; these children lived in Boston. Of the eight children born to the Littles, only Malcolm inherited his mother's light skin color. His hair and skin were sandy brown with reddish overtones. His other siblings had darker coloring. Initially, Malcolm was quite pleased to have a light complexion. In many instances, he could almost pass for white. This light color was much preferred by most African Americans because it was visibly nearer to white and, therefore, more acceptable in society as a whole. Many African American parents tended to treat their lighter-colored children better than their darker ones. This preference for light skin dates back to the slavery tradition of the "mulatto," a person with one white parent and one black.

Growing Up in a Time of Segregation

Malcolm was born at a time when black men and women were little more than second-class citizens. The 1920s were a time of strict segregation under various written and unwritten rules called Jim Crow. According to these "laws," blacks were forbidden to mingle with whites; they were expected to sit in the back of all forms of public transportation; and they were not allowed to use white restrooms or eat in white restaurants. While the Jim Crow laws were most evident in the South, segregation and discrimination were also widespread in the North.

Malcolm lived during the era of Jim Crow laws. These laws segregated blacks from whites in many facets of society, including bus transportation.

Segregation and Discrimination in the North

Legal statutes made segregation the law in the South. While such laws did not exist in the North, racism and discrimination were prevalent in many places. This was called de facto segregation—segregation that existed whether it was legal or not.

Blacks migrated to the North in massive numbers after World War I as they sought freedom and jobs in the factories of the North. Many expected to find the "promised land" there; they expected to be able to live, work, and play with whomever they chose. Historian James H. Cone explains what they found instead: "They found themselves crammed into small ghetto sections of the cities, paying to white landlords and merchants exorbitant prices for rent, food, and clothing, and being policed by white cops who showed no more respect for black life than the white law they knew so well in the South."

Blacks in the North continued to live completely separate lives, as they were forbidden to live in white neighborhoods, denied access to white restaurants and theaters, and faced discrimination in every other aspect of their lives. Unemployment soared as blacks found most factories closed to them. White resentment in numerous northern cities often led to mob violence, urban race riots, and the destruction of entire black communities. The "promised land," in fact, looked a lot like the land they had left behind.

James H. Cone, *Martin and Malcolm and America: A Dream or a Nightmare.* Maryknoll, NY: Orbis, 1992, p. 90.

Living conditions during this time period were often deplorable for blacks; African Americans were restricted from white neighborhoods and, having little money, were forced to live in shantytowns, shacks, and ghettos. Only the most menial and lowest-paying jobs were available, meaning that the majority of blacks lived well below the poverty level.

This strict segregation was often accompanied by racial violence that took the form of murder, untold numbers of lynchings (or hangings), bombings, burnings, and other crimes against the black community. Many of these crimes were committed by the

Ku Klux Klan, a racist terrorist organization that especially targeted blacks who spoke out against the system. Such blacks were labeled troublemakers.

Earl Little

Malcolm's father, in the eyes of the white community, was one such troublemaker. He was a militant follower and member of Marcus Garvey's Back to Africa movement. Garvey believed that blacks were too dependent on whites and needed to create their own businesses and schools. Garvey also advocated that American blacks should separate themselves and move back to what he called their spiritual home of Africa. To implement his plans, Garvey created the Universal Negro Improvement Association.

Malcolm's father, Earl Little, was a militant follower of Marcus Garvey (pictured) and Garvey's Universal Negro Improvement Association.

Earl Little had heard Garvey speak while in Philadelphia and was attracted to the idea of blacks creating their own opportunities. Not content with his place as a second-class citizen, Little took an active role in espousing human rights for blacks. He believed that blacks could not win in the present system of segregation. He took up preaching because it allowed him to speak out for black rights under the protection of the church. His outspokenness, however, made him many enemies.

An incident just prior to Malcolm's birth demonstrates the depth of hatred leveled against Little. Waving torches and rifles and shouting racial obscenities, the Ku Klux Klan visited the Littles' home in Nebraska in the dead of night, surrounded the house, and threatened to lynch Earl Little. Louise Little pleaded with the crowd, telling them that her husband was not home; he

Marcus Garvey

———————◆———————

Marcus Garvey, born in Jamaica in 1887, immigrated to the United States in the 1920s for the purpose of expanding his Universal Negro Improvement Association (UNIA). His primary goal was to promote black pride and foster unity among black people everywhere. He urged self-sufficiency for black communities. Historian William Dudley summarizes: "The goals of the UNIA . . . were the promotion of race pride, independence for colonies in Africa, support for black business, economic and political self-determination of black communities, and economic and political cooperation among blacks throughout the world."

By 1920 Garvey's United Negro Improvement Association had more than four million members worldwide, with branches in dozens of American cities. Advocating that African Americans should return to Africa, Garvey built a steamship line to provide transportation. Before this idea bore fruit, however, Garvey was arrested in 1925 and convicted of mail fraud. Two years later he was deported to Jamaica. He eventually moved to London, where he died in obscurity. Despite his deportation, Garvey's ideas had taken hold in the minds of thousands of black Americans, including Malcolm Little's father.

Quoted in William Dudley, ed., *Opposing Viewpoints: The Civil Rights Movement.* San Diego: Greenhaven, 1996, p. 41.

was at a meeting many miles away. In their apparent disappointment, the Klan broke every window in the house.

Concerned with this rising level of violence and with the hope of finding better conditions in the North, the Littles decided to leave Omaha. They moved to Milwaukee, Wisconsin, for a brief time, then to Albion, Michigan, but finally settled in Lansing, Michigan. Malcolm was four years old at the time.

In 1929 the Littles bought a house in a white neighborhood in Lansing. The neighbors were appalled; they immediately claimed that, by law, the house had to be sold to whites. The Littles, however, refused to move. Not long thereafter, a white mob belonging to a group called the Black Legion surrounded the house. Malcolm later reported that one of his earliest memories was of this night: "Our home was burning down around us. . . . My mother, with the baby in her arms, just made it into the yard before the house crashed in, showering sparks. I remember we were outside in the night in our underwear, crying and yelling our heads off. The white police and firemen came and stood around watching as the house burned down to the ground."[6]

More Violence

Despite this violence, Earl Little was not to be deterred. He built his family a new house in an area some miles away. This new home was a small farm where the Littles grew vegetables and raised a few small animals. The food derived from these sources helped the Littles survive the early years of the Great Depression (1929–1934), a period of great economic hardship for all Americans. Blacks, however, had been one of the groups hardest hit by the fall of the stock market and the rising unemployment rate.

Little, in the meantime, continued to preach Garvey's theories in secret meetings to those who would listen. Malcolm often accompanied his father to these gatherings of the Universal Negro Improvement Association, an organization that urged blacks to stop trying to blend into white society. Malcolm loved to hear his father speak about the injustices done to the black people. As a result, he learned at a very early age about the issues that faced black America.

Despite Little's attempts at secrecy, white racist groups learned of these meetings. While Malcolm was proud of his father for

A follower of Marcus Garvey stands in front of the Garvey Club, where Universal Negro Improvement Association meetings were held. Malcolm Little often accompanied his father, Earl, to such meetings.

speaking out, he was also afraid for him. Historians explain: "Malcolm was raised in a background of ethnic awareness and dignity, but violence was sparked by white racists trying to stop black people such as Reverend Little from preaching about the black cause."[7]

Malcolm's fears were realized in 1931 when several men came to the Little house to tell the family that his father was dead. Little had been found on the trolley tracks; he had apparently been severely beaten and then laid across the tracks, where a trolley had run over him. His body had been nearly cut in half. Malcolm describes that night: "I remember waking up to the sound of my mother's screaming. . . . I saw the police in the living room . . . something terrible had happened to our father. . . . My mother was hysterical."[8]

Hard Times

Little's death left the family in financial difficulty. They received no benefits from Little's life insurance policy after his death. Based on police reports, the insurance company, which was owned and managed by whites, ruled that Little had committed suicide. As a result, because the insurance policy did not pay off for suicidal death, the family struggled to make ends meet. Malcolm reported that on many occasions all they had to eat was a bowl of cornmeal or dandelion greens.

And yet the large family managed to survive with the help of friends and neighbors who gave them food and clothing. In addition, Louise Little joined the Seventh-Day Adventist Church, which also helped them with meals. Malcolm and another brother contributed by hunting bullfrogs and rabbits, which could be used to prepare stews and soups.

Malcolm's mother also found whatever jobs she could. These were mostly cleaning and sewing for the white families of Lansing. She often worked eight- to ten-hour days, earning no more than fifty cents for a day's work. She also found a job as a salesclerk in a white store, passing for white because of her light skin. When the employer discovered that she had black children, however, she was fired. Little also received a welfare check and a widow's pension, but her total income was never enough to support the family.

Like this woman, Malcolm's mother Louise struggled to support her family with jobs such as cleaning and sewing for white families.

Because the family never had enough money to pay the bills, welfare workers became constant visitors to the Little home. They told the family they were concerned about whether the children were getting enough to eat and had adequate clothing. The children quickly began to resent the welfare workers' questions about their mother. According to Malcolm, the workers also questioned each child individually and occasionally tried to convince the children their mother was unfit to raise them. Malcolm just wanted to be left alone.

The Little Family Is Broken Apart

While times were hard for the entire family, it was Louise Little who was impacted the most. Forced to assume the role of the head of the family, she seemed lost at times and completely overwhelmed. She spent hours crying over her inability to take care of her children.

Louise, faced with this overwhelming responsibility and depression, began talking to herself and drifting away to a fantasy world where conditions were better. It became increasingly scary for the children to watch their mother's mental status deteriorate. As the welfare workers increased their visits, they talked more and more about splitting up the family. Malcolm, little more than ten years old, was terrified at what was happening to his family. He had trouble sleeping at night and hated the visits made by the state welfare people.

To help compensate for these feelings, Malcolm began hanging out with a wild group of youngsters who turned to small-time stealing—primarily candy and fruit from the grocery store. The Lansing area courts took a dim view of such activity, however, and maintained that Louise could no longer control or adequately care for her children.

When Malcolm was thirteen, his mother was declared insane and was committed to a mental hospital, where she stayed for the next twenty-six years. The Little children were split up and sent to live with various families in the community. "I truly believe that if ever a state social agency destroyed a family, it destroyed ours,"[9] Malcolm wrote in his autobiography. He also told reporters years later: "We were state children, court wards; the judge had the full say-so over us. A white man in charge of a black man's children. Nothing but legal, modern slavery."[10]

Malcolm, in his first thirteen years, had seen more violence and disruption than most people experience in a lifetime. He had been pulled out of his home while it burned down around him. He had been exposed to the violent death of his father at the hands of white racists. He had also seen the slow mental and emotional breakdown of his mother. Finally, he had been separated from his brothers and sisters.

Detention

After his mother was sent away, Malcolm lived for a while with the Gohannas family, an older white couple who received a fee for taking in troubled children. He was very unhappy with the whole situation and stopped applying himself in school. He became the class clown and started making smart comments to his teachers. His behavior in school became disruptive and, after he was caught putting thumbtacks on the chair of his teacher, he was eventually expelled and placed in a juvenile detention center.

The place he was sent to was run by a white couple named Swerlin. They apparently took a liking to Malcolm and arranged for the youngster to stay with them rather than be sent to a reform school. Despite their kindness, however, the Swerlins were just as prejudiced as other whites in the area. Within Malcolm's hearing, they talked derisively about blacks. The general opinion among most whites during this time period was that the majority of African Americans were inferior in every way to whites.

Mr. Swerlin, for example, once asked his wife how the blacks could be so happy when they were so poor. Mrs. Swerlin responded that that was just the way they were. These comments disturbed Malcolm, and he seethed inside, being unable to correct the Swerlins' impressions. The worst part for Malcolm was that the Swerlins talked of these things in his presence. He came to believe that the couple must have thought he was too stupid to understand what they were talking about. Malcolm would later tell friends that the Swerlins had treated him more like a pet animal than a human being.

Nonetheless, he stayed with the Swerlins and was enrolled in a new school, Mason Junior High School, composed primarily of whites. He quickly learned to harden himself against the racial slurs that he heard daily. On the surface, he got along well with

While in foster care, Malcolm Little attended a desegregated high school, like the one pictured here.

his classmates, but he knew he was popular because he was black and different. Despite his so-called popularity, all his friends used derogatory terms to refer to other black people. So, too, did many of Malcolm's teachers. Malcolm recalls the day his class learned about African American history. The students were told to open their textbook to the section on African American history, which was covered in one brief paragraph. The teacher laughed as he told the students that, while free, Negroes were usually dumb and could not be trusted.

Despite these underlying conflicts, Malcolm liked school and improved his grades, bringing his class rank up to third. He was also elected president of his seventh-grade class. He played basketball for the school team but was forced to endure more racial slurs when playing in other gymnasiums. Malcolm also often attended school dances but was then forced to stand around and watch his classmates dance; he, like other blacks elsewhere, was forbidden to dance with white girls.

Ella and a Trip to Boston

Malcolm, while living with the Swerlins, still managed to stay in touch with his brothers and sisters. He saw them nearly every weekend. During one weekend, he met his half sister Ella for the first time; she was Earl Little's daughter by his first marriage. Malcolm was very impressed with her and wrote, "She was the first really proud black woman I had ever seen in my life."[11] Malcolm enjoyed the time he spent with Ella. When she returned to Boston, she invited Malcolm to visit her.

During the summer of 1940, when Malcolm was fifteen, he caught a Greyhound bus and went to Boston. Malcolm was awestruck by everything he saw and witnessed. Ella lived in the Roxbury section of Boston, a middle-class black neighborhood. It was unlike anything Malcolm had ever seen. For the first time Malcolm saw blacks living in nice homes, wearing new clothes, driving cars, and having good educations. He saw them eating in nice restaurants. He was amazed at the amount of freedom these northeastern blacks seemed to have.

He was reluctant to leave Boston, but he had to return to school in Michigan. He was restless when he returned, not being able to get thoughts of Boston out of his head. He yearned to return.

In the meantime, however, Malcolm continued school. He had a meeting with his English teacher and adviser, whom he liked and respected. The teacher asked Malcolm if he had been considering what he wanted to do with his life, what kind of career he wanted to pursue. "Well, sir,"

A young Malcolm poses for a photo in the 1930s. Although separated from his brothers and sisters as a child, Malcolm managed to stay in contact with them and with his half sister, Ella, who lived in Boston.

Malcolm responded, "I've been thinking I'd like to be a lawyer." The teacher looked surprised and said: "Don't misunderstand me. We all here like you, you know that. But you've got to be realistic. . . . A lawyer—that's no realistic goal for [a black person] . . . you're good with your hands . . . why don't you plan on carpentry?"[12] Malcolm's hopes plummeted. Historian Peter Goldman summarizes: "In the eighth grade, he collided with the fact . . . that the black children of Middle America . . . did not dare risk having ambitions or dreams."[13]

Malcolm was hurt and disappointed, for he knew that the same teacher had urged white teenagers to do more and reach for higher goals despite the fact that their grades were far beneath those that Malcolm had. This incident caused Malcolm to change, and he began to draw away from his white teachers and classmates. The same racist remarks that he had ignored now began to hurt and bother him. He later stated the remarks hurt because he had seen how blacks lived elsewhere.

Malcolm began writing more and more letters to Ella in Boston. He eventually told her that he would like to live in Boston. After obtaining permission from the state welfare system, Ella was granted custody of Malcolm, and in 1940 he made his arrangements to leave Michigan and move to Boston. He was fifteen years old.

Chapter Two

"Detroit Red"

By the time Malcolm moved in with his half sister, Ella had separated from her husband and was living alone. She provided Malcolm with his own room and set about introducing her brother to her friends and colleagues.

He describes the blacks he met from Ella's neighborhood: "I saw those Roxbury Negroes acting and living differently from any black people I'd ever dreamed of in my life. This was the snooty-black neighborhood; they called themselves the 'Four Hundred,' and looked down their noses at the Negroes of the black ghetto."[14]

Malcolm saw that these blacks were trying very hard to be "white" or at least to imitate whites. In actual fact, however, most of the Roxbury Negroes worked in menial jobs with low pay. When a black man claimed that he was "in banking," the reality was often that he worked as a janitor in a bank. Likewise, a black woman who bragged she came from a wealthy family often meant she worked as a servant for a rich white family. Malcolm hated this kind of hypocrisy.

Malcolm, as a result, was not interested in friendships with the blacks who lived in Roxbury. He thought many of Ella's friends were shallow and trying hard to be something they were not—white. He, instead, sought out other blacks who lived in other areas of Boston. Spurning many of Ella's invitations, Malcolm began to explore the "other side" of Roxbury—the pool halls and neighborhood bars. Malcolm describes what he found: "That world of grocery stores, walk-up flats, cheap restaurants, poolrooms, bars, storefront churches, and pawnshops seemed to hold a natural lure for me."[15]

One of the first people that Malcolm met was an older teenager named "Shorty" Jarvis, who was also from the Lansing, Michigan, area. They became instant friends. Discovering that he was quite naive in the ways of this "new" world of pawnshops,

This is the Roxbury house where Malcolm lived with his half sister, Ella, during his years in Boston.

bars, and poolrooms, Malcolm slowly began to learn his way around with Shorty's help.

Roseland Ballroom

At age fifteen, Malcolm was well over 6 feet (1.8m) tall and looked older than his age. He wanted people to think he was older, so he developed a confident swagger in his walk. Shorty helped him find his first job—shining shoes at the Roseland Ballroom, a whites-only dance hall. Malcolm learned the trade from Freddie, the young man he was replacing. Malcolm soon realized that Freddie had made less money shining shoes than he did by selling liquor and marijuana, as well as arranging visits with black prostitutes for white men. Malcolm quickly learned how to please and service everyone, whether they wanted alcohol, women, or drugs. He received large tips for these extra services.

While the ballroom was for whites only, many of the finest black bands in the world played there, including those of the well-known Count Basie, Lionel Hampton, and Duke Ellington. Watching the dancers each night, Malcolm yearned to dance himself. He soon quit the job at the ballroom and began attending other dances where blacks were allowed. He loved to dance and was soon quite good at it, dancing with all the most popular girls. He practiced in front of a mirror and specialized in the Lindy Hop, a dance craze of the late 1930s and early 1940s that involved jumps, shouts, and gyrations.

Cool and Hip

Financing his dancing became a problem, so Malcolm began to look for another job. Ella got him his next job as a soda fountain clerk in a fashionable part of Roxbury. While there, he met a well-educated black girl named Laura. Malcolm frequently took Laura dancing; she, like Ella, told Malcolm that if he committed himself to learning, he could still be a lawyer. Malcolm, however, had lost interest in this goal and was content with his current lifestyle. Laura was hopeful that the relationship with Malcolm would turn serious, but he was not interested in a commitment. He admitted freely that he was more intent on getting his "kicks," and he soon broke up with Laura and began attending dances with a white woman named Sophia. After the dances, the two frequented various bars in the Boston area. People noticed. The interracial relationship drew stares and gained Malcolm prestige among his black companions.

In order to fit his prestigious image, Malcolm also began to change his dress and appearance to appear "cool" and more "hip." With his first paychecks, he bought himself a "zoot suit," featuring wide shoulders and baggy pants. He also bought himself a pair of yellow-toed shoes.

In addition to his new attire, Malcolm wanted to get rid of his kinky hair. With Shorty's help, he "conked" it, straightening it by using a painful process to get the kinks out. Malcolm utilized a homemade concoction of lye and potatoes. The solution was so potent that it burned his scalp, but he knew that the longer the mixture was on, the straighter his hair would become. Despite the pain, he was quite satisfied with the results—it made him look less like a black man.

Malcolm, in addition to changing his appearance, also began to develop some bad habits. He started drinking alcohol, smoking cigarettes, and even tried his first reefers (marijuana cigarettes). The use of alcohol and cigarettes coincided with his hanging out with Shorty and his friends, playing pool, gambling, and playing the numbers. Playing the numbers refers to betting on a three-digit number, something that thousands of blacks did. A hit or win meant correctly guessing the last three numbers of the New York Stock Exchange's printed total of domestic and foreign sales.

As a result of his new lifestyle, Malcolm and Ella began having difficulties. She did not approve of his continuing relationship with Sophia, nor did she like his new appearance and new habits. She disapproved wholeheartedly of his friendships with Shorty and others. At the same time, Malcolm became restless and decided to go to the Harlem area of New York City, a place his father had often spoken of with pride.

Harlem

The year was 1942, and war had just broken out with Japan and Germany. Many jobs were available because so many men had entered the armed forces, but at the age of sixteen, Malcolm was still too young for the army. He eventually got a job on the New Haven and Hartford Yankee Clipper train that traveled between

Boston and New York. He worked in the dining car, washing dishes, selling sandwiches, and cleaning up the kitchen.

During his layovers in New York, he visited the Harlem area of the city, a vibrant and busy black metropolis. Malcolm quickly fell in love with the area and found himself a small boardinghouse room to rent. He began spending most of his evenings at Small's Paradise, a famous Harlem nightspot and a hangout for many Harlem criminals. He hung around the bar and met many colorful individuals with names such as "West Indian Archie," "Sammy the

During layovers from his job on the Yankee Clipper train, Malcolm spent many of his evenings at Small's Paradise, a famous Harlem nightspot and hangout for criminals.

Pimp," "Dollarbill," and "Few Clothes." Malcolm soon received his own nicknames: "Detroit Red," because of his Michigan upbringing and his red hair; and "Big Red," because of his size.

While working at Small's as a waiter, he was offered another job, that of a runner for a numbers man. Malcolm became one of

Harlem

■

Harlem began as a Dutch settlement and was home to wave after wave of European immigrants before becoming a predominantly black area of New York in the early twentieth century. By the 1920s, Harlem had become the center of black music and entertainment, as well as other creative arts.

The area was financially supported by white New Yorkers who flocked by the thousands into Harlem every night to listen to outstanding black musicians. The whites also came to dance in such places as the Savoy Ballroom with its 200-foot (61m) dance floor. Other famous nightspots included the Cotton Club and the Apollo and Lafayette theaters.

Harlem's great popularity among whites began to ebb after the stock market crash in 1929. The economic situation in Harlem became dire during the Great Depression, leading to the growth of illegal activity of all kinds—the same kinds that Malcolm Little found appealing.

The growing sense of desperation in Harlem exploded in 1943 when a black soldier was shot to death in Harlem by a white policeman. Riots ensued, and hundreds of people were injured and five killed. By the time the riot ended, Harlem's business district lay in ruins, leaving the community—and the economy—devastated.

An overturned vehicle burns during the 1943 Harlem Riots. By the time the riots ended, Harlem's community and its economy were in ruins.

many people collecting tickets for the illegal lottery game run by New York mobsters. Malcolm worked for a controller, who probably had as many as fifty runners collecting money from people all across Harlem. Runners usually earned 10 percent of whatever money they turned in.

A Life of Crime

From that point on, Malcolm's life descended into a world of crime. He not only was involved in the numbers business but also sold bootleg, or illegal, whiskey as well as hot, or stolen, goods.

In addition to being involved in these crimes, Malcolm began to use cocaine and marijuana. He liked the cocaine because it made him feel more in control of himself. He generally obtained the drugs from merchant seamen who visited New York. Because the drugs were so available, Malcolm also began selling them on the streets of Harlem.

Because of his various criminal associations and the deals he was making on the street, Malcolm began carrying a gun. He learned money was to be made in gambling and began playing poker and blackjack at Grand Central Station. By 1943 he was under surveillance by the New York City police. It did not take long for the narcotic detectives to realize Malcolm was selling marijuana. They began to follow him. Malcolm's life became a game of cat and mouse as he moved from one cheap boardinghouse to another, trying to evade the police.

Finding it difficult to continue selling drugs because of the police surveillance, Malcolm turned to robbery. He made his money from holding up small liquor stores and drugstores in the Harlem area and elsewhere. Malcolm later stated that he felt no remorse about robbing white people. He believed that in a white-dominated society, a black man had to find a way to make money, even if it involved criminal activity. He also robbed people on the street to get money for his ever-growing drug habit.

Historian Michael Friedly summarizes Malcolm's lifestyle:

> The gun-toting teenager involved himself in the criminal underworld where death by natural causes was the exception and not the norm. . . . He cultivated the reputation of a crazy, trigger-happy punk who cared no more for his own

life than he did for those he threatened to kill. . . . At one point, he loaded his pistol with a single bullet, put the gun to his head and pulled the trigger in an attempt to show his fellow burglars that they must not be afraid to die.[16]

By late 1943 Malcolm was also living in constant fear of Harlem's underworld mobsters. He was beaten up on at least one occasion by mobsters who were not happy with Malcolm's drug dealing and other crimes; he was infringing on their territory. He was also caught cheating at cards. One of his old friends, West Indian Archie, swore he would kill Malcolm. Malcolm barely escaped with his life, and only with the help of Shorty, who arrived and spirited him out of New York.

Arrest and Conviction

Leaving New York, Malcolm moved back to Boston and resumed his life of crime. He quickly became involved in gambling and

Dodging the Draft

In addition to dodging the police wherever he went, by the time he turned eighteen in 1943 Malcolm was also trying to avoid the draft. With World War II still raging in Europe and the Pacific, he needed to register for the draft and enter the armed forces. Malcolm was determined not to serve and devised a way to avoid the draft.

Malcolm, by this time, was quite the con man. He easily convinced the army doctors that he was unfit for duty. As part of the physical examination given by the army, Malcolm talked to a psychiatrist. He put on the performance of his life.

In addition to looking under closet doors for an intruder, Malcolm kept up a rapid chatter that made no sense. Malcolm told the psychiatrist: "Daddy-o, now you and me, we're from up North here. So don't you tell nobody. . . . I want to get sent down South. Organize them . . . soldiers, you dig? Steal us some guns, and kill us crackers." The psychiatrist quickly marked Malcolm down as unfit for duty.

Malcolm X with Alex Haley, *The Autobiography of Malcolm X*. New York: Grove, 1964, p. 108.

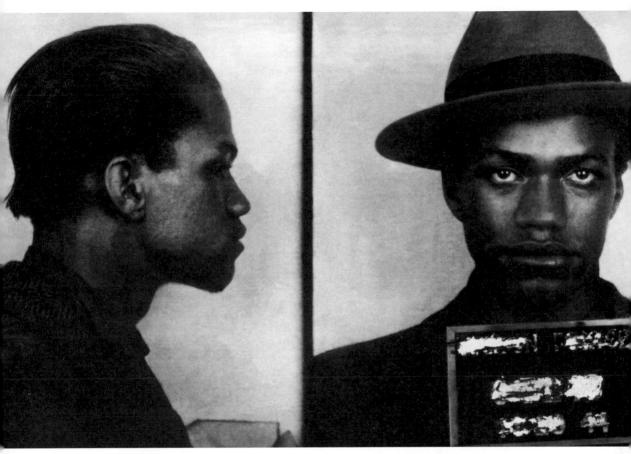

Malcolm Little's mug shot, taken after his arrest for burglary in Boston during the 1940s.

numbers running in Roxbury. He also organized a robbery ring with Shorty. They robbed corner drugstores and liquor stores in the Boston area. After finding that these targets did not result in much cash flow, he and Shorty turned to robbing homes. Having kept up his relationship with Sophia while in New York, Malcolm enlisted her help and that of her sister to scout out potential targets. The women were sent ahead to check out the houses to see if anybody were home. The men then robbed the homes and sold the goods to a pawnbroker.

Malcolm was eventually caught by the police after leaving a stolen watch at a jewelry store to be repaired. The store recognized the piece and notified police, who were waiting to arrest him when he came to pick up the watch. Malcolm readily admitted that he had lived a charmed existence, avoiding the police for as long as he had. Goldman elaborates: "His police record, given the energy and variety of his criminal life, stayed remarkably clean: it shows arrests for larceny in Michigan and burglary in Massachusetts, but none at all—not even a traffic ticket—in New York."[17]

His luck, however, had run out. Malcolm was twenty years old when he stood before the judge and heard the verdict and sentence. He was convicted of fourteen different counts of burglary. A first offense such as Malcolm's normally earned a two-year sentence, but Malcolm received ten years. The year was 1946, and he had not even begun shaving when his sentence was passed. The presiding judge told Malcolm that this time in prison would teach him to stay away from white girls. Most historians, as well as Malcolm himself, believe that going to prison probably saved his life. Had he continued his life of crime, he told reporters later, the mobsters would have eventually killed him.

Malcolm Goes to Prison

Malcolm began his prison sentence at Charlestown Prison in Massachusetts, a rundown facility that had been built in 1805. He was placed in a tiny cell with no running water and only a covered bucket to serve as a toilet. He was deprived of drugs and underwent a harrowing and painful withdrawal from cocaine.

He, like other prisoners, was forced to endure the prison's dreary daily schedule of confinement and limited exercise. Never referred to by his name, he was given a prison number and addressed in that manner throughout his incarceration at Charlestown. He later told reporters that he felt like a caged animal. He reacted by becoming even more defiant, often throwing loud temper tantrums. As a result of these outbursts, Malcolm frequently spent time in solitary confinement. Rather than reforming his ways, though, Malcolm liked being an outcast and was soon given the nickname of "Satan" by his fellow prisoners because of his hostility toward religion and prison life in general.

Malcolm quickly learned to work around the rules and soon found out that drugs were in fact available for the right price. He used the cash that Ella sent him, intended for other purposes, to buy drugs. He, like many of the other prisoners, also drank a spiced drink made of nutmeg and water that produced a marijuana-like high. He made additional money working as a bookie at Charlestown, arranging for other inmates' bets on horse races and boxing matches. He also wanted no part of the counseling services available at the prison and refused talks with the psychologist and chaplain, because he did not think he needed help.

Enlightenment

Malcolm may very well have continued to act out against the system had he not met another prisoner who helped him turn his life around. Malcolm took his first steps toward changing his behavior after meeting an older prisoner named John Elton Bembry, known as "Bimbi," a professional burglar serving a long sentence. Bimbi told Malcolm that he had used his own prison time to improve his education by studying and reading. Malcolm listened to Bimbi because of the respect shown to the older prisoner by the other inmates.

He had met Bimbi in a prison workshop where they worked side by side making license plates. After listening to Malcolm make a derogatory remark about religion, Bimbi told Malcolm that he was shortsighted and did not know what he was talking about. Bimbi challenged Malcolm to use the prison library to learn about religion and other subjects.

Bimbi's challenge must have made a deep impression on the young Malcolm, who began using the library and even took a few distance-learning courses through the mail. He also began attending a few classes at the prison school. Since Malcolm had attended regular school only through the eighth grade, he knew he still needed to do a lot of learning.

In the reading he did, what impressed Malcolm the most was black history. He spent long hours learning about the historical treatment of blacks by whites. The more he read, the more outraged he became, especially about slavery and the effects of that institution on African Americans. He was also fascinated by what he read about the great African civilizations that had existed prior to the colonization of Africa and the arrival of the white man. What he read reinforced many of his ideas about the white man and the injustices done to black Americans. "I knew right there

Malcolm served his sentence for burglary in the Charlestown Prison (pictured) in Massachusetts. While incarcerated, Malcolm began reading books on black history that changed his views forever.

in prison that reading had changed forever the course of my life," Malcolm later wrote. "As I see it today, the ability to read awoke inside me some long dormant craving to be mentally alive."[18]

Malcolm began reading late into the night, using only a pale light in the hall for illumination. As a result of this poor lighting,

Malcolm would eventually need glasses. He became so absorbed by what he was reading that he slept only three or four hours a night.

Transfer to Norfolk

Around this same time, in 1948, Ella, at Malcolm's request, arranged for him to be transferred to Norfolk Prison, a more modern and much cleaner facility. Norfolk was a new kind of prison, an experimental jail with a focus on rehabilitating prisoners for their reentry into society.

Norfolk also had a much bigger library, which Malcolm used frequently. In an effort to improve his mind and his writing skills, he began copying the dictionary word for word. This vastly improved his penmanship and his knowledge. When he started his self-improvement program, Malcolm estimated that he had a

Norfolk Prison Debating Program

Norfolk Prison had opened in 1931 under the leadership of Superintendent Howard B. Gill. Journalist Robert James Branham explains Gill's philosophy: "[He] sought to create a physical and social environment that could counter the negative influences that had shaped the inmate's prior life." Instead of living in a locked cell, each prisoner had his own room in a dormitory where no doors were locked. And the educational opportunities were vast.

The weekly Norfolk debates attracted large audiences from the Boston area. If the subject matter being debated related to the government, for instance, various government representatives were present. Malcolm Little became one of Norfolk Prison's most eloquent debaters. Regardless of which side of the question he was supposed to take, Malcolm read and studied the subject and was well prepared to debate the issue.

As a result of the debating program, Malcolm became a dynamic speaker. Branham explains: "It was in the extraordinary debating program . . . that Malcolm X gained the training and experience in public speaking that would have a profound influence on his later career."

Robert James Branham, "'I Was Gone on Debating': Malcolm X's Prison Debates and Public Confrontations," *Argumentation and Advocacy*, January 1, 1995.

working vocabulary of only a few hundred words. His handwriting was so poor that he could barely write in a straight line. Toward the end of his prison term, both had improved dramatically.

He continued his reading, which only reinforced his already negative image of the white man. He began teaching his fellow black inmates about what he had read, especially the issues revolving around slavery, segregation, and discrimination. He also began to enter the prison colony's weekly debating program. It was his first introduction to public speaking, and he discovered he had some natural skills.

Malcolm often spoke of the debating as an important part of his reeducation. He stated: "I will tell you right there, in the prison, debating, speaking to a crowd, was as exhilarating to me as the discovery of knowledge through reading had been."[19] It was through this program that Malcolm began his preparations for a career of public speaking.

Chapter Three

Minister Malcolm X

In addition to his self-education about black history and his success in the debating program at Norfolk Prison, Malcolm also took his first steps toward a religious awakening. His brothers Reginald and Philbert, as well as his sister Hilda, were all members of the Nation of Islam, a Muslim religion for African Americans. They began talking to Malcolm about the importance of religious belief. In the beginning, Malcolm scoffed at the idea and was sarcastic about their faith, but he also began to listen to their words.

He decided to expand his reading program in order to understand fully what his siblings were talking about. He began to read everything he could find in the prison library about the Nation of Islam and its charismatic leader, Elijah Muhammad.

The Nation of Islam and Black Nationalism

One of the first things that Malcolm discovered in his reading was that the Nation of Islam was the leading voice of black nationalism. Historian James H. Cone explains: "For nationalists, freedom was not black people pleading for integration into white society; rather, it was separation from white people so that blacks could govern themselves."[20]

Malcolm was further fascinated to learn that Marcus Garvey of the United Negro Improvement Association was considered the grandfather of black nationalism. As he read more about the man his father had idolized and supported, he remembered the many meetings he had attended as a child. In addition to urging blacks to return to their homeland in Africa, Garvey also had been an ardent supporter of the concept of blacks separating themselves from whites in all aspects of life.

In addition to Garvey, Malcolm learned, the early 1900s also had produced the Moorish Science Temple of America, founded by Timothy Drew. Trained in mysticism, Drew, who called himself Noble Drew Ali, the Prophet, claimed that blacks originated in the Middle East and were formerly Islamic. Drew espoused a theory that blacks were superior to whites and that the white race

was doomed. His organization drew nearly fifteen thousand followers before a power struggle resulted in the division of the organization into two separate groups. One of these was the Nation of Islam, or Black Muslims, as its members also were called. The other group remained the Moorish Science Temple.

The Nation of Islam had been founded by a door-to-door silk salesman named Wallace D. Fard, who proclaimed himself a god. According to Fard, the mission of the Nation of Islam was to "teach the downtrodden and defenseless black people a thorough knowledge of God and of themselves, and to put them on the road to

Wallace D. Fard, founder of the Nation of Islam, poses for a photo. Malcolm believed in many of Fard's ideas and eventually joined his organization.

Wallace D. Fard

Wallace D. Fard sold products door to door for a living, but he styled himself a prophet who had come to America to help blacks discover their true nature. In 1930 he founded the Nation of Islam, then known as the Temple of Islam, in Detroit, Michigan. His preaching emphasized the superiority of the black race along with a mythical interpretation of the creation of the world.

Historian Peter Goldman summarizes: "God, it is written, appeared to the black people of Detroit's Paradise Valley slums on July 4, 1930." God had apparently taken the form of Wallace D. Fard, who acquired a small circle of followers who initially met secretly in basements and shacks. When asked who he was, Fard replied: "I am the one the world has been expecting for the past two thousand years. . . . My name is Mahdi; I am God. I came to guide you into the right path that you may be successful and see the hereafter."

In 1934 Fard disappeared and was never heard from again, although his followers believed he had continued his ministry elsewhere. Fard's number one student, Elijah Muhammad, took control of the Nation of Islam and continued Fard's teaching.

Peter Goldman, *The Death and Life of Malcolm X*. Urbana: University of Illinois Press, 1979, pp. 35, 36.

self-independence with a superior culture and higher civilization than they had previously experienced."[21]

Two major principles guided the Nation of Islam. The first was black pride, meaning that all African Americans should consider themselves racially and socially superior to whites, and the second was black self-sufficiency. The Nation's ministers advocated black economic, social, cultural, and political independence from white society. These principles were based on the underlying belief that blacks were the original people on earth and were, as a result, far superior to the white race.

Malcolm read that Black Muslims believed that all white people were corrupt and dishonest and, therefore, were the source of all evil in the world. Whites were, thus, solely responsible for the oppression of Africans throughout the world.

These ideas resonated deeply within Malcolm Little. He had seen proof of the white man's evil throughout his childhood. Whites had been responsible for burning his home, murdering his father, and splitting up his family. Everywhere Malcolm had gone in the ghettos of Boston and New York he had also seen evidence of black oppression. It was easy for Malcolm to believe that the white man had been responsible for many of his own problems.

Elijah Muhammad

Malcolm next turned to reading about the current leader of the Nation of Islam, Elijah Muhammad. While Fard was the founder of the Nation, Muhammad was often credited with many of the Black Muslim doctrines and practices. Calling himself "The Messenger," Muhammad preached a doctrine that stated: "History had been whitened in the white man's history book, and . . . the black man had been brainwashed for hundreds of years"[22] into believing they were second-class citizens.

Elijah Muhammad, Malcolm learned, had been born Elijah Poole in rural Georgia in 1897. He was one of twelve children born to a black minister and had a fourth-grade education. In 1919 Elijah married Clara Evans, referred to later as Mother Clara Muhammad, and together the couple had eight children. Early in his marriage, he worked for the railroad and also a brick company. Looking for a better life, he and his family moved to Detroit in 1923 to work on the automobile assembly line.

In 1930 Poole met Fard, the founder of the Nation (or Temple) of Islam. Fard taught Poole about his version of the Islamic faith and his theories of the evolution and superiority of the black race. Poole took the name Elijah Muhammad and became Fard's chief aide and most devoted disciple. He chose the name Muhammad in honor of the Prophet Muhammad, the founder of the Muslim faith as practiced in the Middle East. By ridding himself of his original name, Elijah believed he was throwing off his slave name.

Eventually, Muhammad and Fard moved to Chicago, where they founded a new temple. Together they saw growing support for their organization in the 1930s. Their message of black superiority was very appealing to the poor blacks in the northern ghettos. When Fard mysteriously disappeared not long thereafter, Muhammad took over the leadership of the Nation of Islam.

Although he did not found the Nation of Islam, leader Elijah Muhammad was considered the person most responsible for shaping the movement's ideas.

At this time, Malcolm read, Muhammad set about trying to increase the membership of the Nation of Islam. He and his ministers began preaching the message of black power to African Americans living in the ghettos and prisons. It was through the prison ministry of the organization, as well as the work of his brothers and sister, that Malcolm Little heard about Muhammad and the Nation.

While Malcolm was emotionally moved by what he had read, the white press condemned the Nation of Islam and its followers. *Time* magazine ran an editorial in 1961 that stated: "While their leaders, protected by shaved-head honor guards, are preaching cold hatred . . . in principal United States cities, lesser Muslim agents are at work in many a United States prison, spreading fanatical doctrines and recruiting new brethren among Negro prisoners. . . . Prisons are a natural breeding ground for the hate group."[23] Even many black spokesmen were critical of the Nation: Supreme Court justice Thurgood Marshall, the first African American to sit on the Court, denounced the Black Muslims, claiming they were "being run by a bunch of thugs organized

The Gospel According to Fard

Wallace D. Fard taught that God, or Allah, had created mankind in God's image—and God was black. Black scientists, at Allah's request, made the mountains, the valleys, and the seas.

Fard taught that evil had entered the world due to a mad scientist named Yacub, whose pride had led him to break Islamic laws. He was exiled from the promised land and, in revenge, created the white race. Allah sent the black prophets Moses and Jesus to teach the whites about Islam, but the whites corrupted the message and created Judaism and Christianity instead. The white devils, Fard preached, eventually gained control of the world and created slavery, which was ordained to last four hundred years.

Fard also taught that at the end of six thousand years, which was to arrive early in the twenty-first century, the white race would be destroyed. At that time, a man-made planet called the Mother Ship would descend from space and call all blacks to come on board. Any blacks who chose not to enter would be condemned to die with the whites in a series of natural disasters that would devastate Earth. For the next one thousand years, according to Fard, no life would exist on Earth. Then the children of the Original People, or blacks, would return and recivilize the planet.

This tale not only infuriated whites but also enraged Islamic leaders throughout the world. This was not the story that the Islamic prophet Muhammad had brought to the world in ancient times.

from prisons and jails."[24] The followers of traditional Islam were also critical of the Nation of Islam and its practices.

A Religious Conversion

Despite these negative remarks, the reading Malcolm had done had opened his mind in a spiritual way. When he read the Nation of Islam's message, he felt for the first time a spark of inner pride about being a black man. He also began finding a sense of hope and peace about his future.

In addition to the letters he received and sent to his siblings, in late 1949 Malcolm began corresponding with Elijah Muhammad. He read and reread these letters, and found his heart and soul responding to Muhammad's words of encouragement. He decided to join the Nation of Islam. He also adopted the habits of Black Muslims; he stopped smoking, drinking, and using drugs, because the Nation wanted their members to be pure. The Nation also viewed these habits as something the white people had introduced. For Malcolm, giving up these habits meant a commitment to leading a life without the addictions that helped get him into trouble.

He then started a letter-writing campaign from prison. As a member of the Nation of Islam, he wrote to numerous government officials demanding an end to racism and prejudice. He also organized discussion groups with other prisoners; during the group meetings, he spoke about the Nation of Islam and the plight of the black man. He was responsible for helping recruit dozens of new members to the faith.

Malcolm X

During the spring of 1952, the Massachusetts Parole Board voted that Malcolm should be released from prison for good behavior. He had served seven years of his ten-year sentence in three different prisons; he was twenty-seven years old. He would be on parole for the remainder of the original sentence, but would remain free as long as he stayed out of trouble and kept in contact with his parole officer.

Malcolm decided not to return to either Boston or Harlem and instead went to the Detroit area where his brothers and sisters lived. Once there, he was given a job in a furniture store managed by his brother Wilfred. He dressed in a style used by the men who belonged to the Nation of Islam; he kept his hair short and wore black suits, white shirts, and slender black ties.

On Labor Day, 1952, Malcolm met Elijah Muhammad for the first time. He was completely overwhelmed with the presence of the leader of the Nation of Islam. Muhammad praised Malcolm for his strength and his adherence to Muslim traditions while in prison. Malcolm reports on this meeting: "I was totally unprepared for the Messenger Elijah Muhammad's physical impact upon my emotions. . . . I sat, leaning forward, riveted upon his words."[25]

Muhammad urged Malcolm to take a new name. Most surnames of African Americans had been given to a family member during the period of slavery and were generally that of the white owner. For the Nation of Islam, these names were, therefore, considered meaning-less. Members of the Nation often used the letter "X," which symbolized the unknown African names of their ancestors. For Malcolm, taking the name X became his final step in becoming a new person after all the years he had spent in crime and in prison. Malcolm X pledged to devote his life to the Nation of Islam and to Allah. He believed that Elijah Muhammad and his teachings had saved him.

The Message of Minister Malcolm X

With his new identity, Malcolm X began attending services and meetings at Temple Number One in Detroit. Because of the good speaking skills he had learned in prison, Malcolm's first job was that of recruiting new members for the temple. Recruiting, in Black Muslim terminology, was often referred to as "going fishing" —fishing for souls. Within a few months, Temple Number One had more than tripled its membership.

Malcolm would eventually become one of the Nation's best recruiters and was responsible for bringing thousands of new members into the temple. His best work was done in the ghettos where he met people one-on-one and spoke to them of the message Elijah Muhammad sent. Malcolm was a natural leader; his charm and charisma mesmerized listeners who heard his speeches.

While preaching about the goodness of Allah, he also campaigned against the white man. He spoke often of the history of black slavery and how the white man had made the black man a second-class citizen. Malcolm was soon attracting large crowds

After meeting Elijah Muhammad (right) in 1952, Malcolm Little (left) decided to change his name to Malcolm X and to devote his life to the Nation of Islam.

wherever he went because he was speaking the words that so many other black people felt they could not say. Their voices had been silent due to fear of white reprisals.

Malcolm's message appealed especially to the poor blacks who lived in American ghettos, where oppression and poverty were the worst. In an interview given in 1963, he talked about Muslim converts:

> At the bottom of the heap is the black man in the big-city ghetto. He lives night and day with the rats and cock-roaches and drowns himself with alcohol and anesthetizes himself with dope, to try and forget where and what he is. That Negro has given up all hope. He's the hardest one for us to reach, because he's the deepest in the mud. But when you get him . . . he's the most fearless. He will stand the longest. He has nothing to lose, not even his life, because he didn't have that in the first place.[26]

Malcolm was rewarded for his work by being named the assistant minister at Temple Number One in Detroit. He had never imagined that he would one day become a minister for any religion. Malcolm had truly found his calling. From Detroit, Malcolm was sent in 1954 to open a new temple in Boston. In many ways, his return to Boston was a homecoming. He reconnected with Ella, although she was not entirely pleased with his choice of religion. Malcolm would eventually win her over and convince her to convert to Islam. He also saw many of his old friends, most of whom were still involved in criminal acts and behavior. They, in particular, were amazed at the changes he had made, while Malcolm was concerned that his friends had not changed at all.

After the Boston temple was up and running, Malcolm was sent to Philadelphia for a period of three months to start Temple Number Twelve. From there he returned to New York, where he was given the job of minister at Temple Number Seven in Harlem. He returned to the streets of Harlem, this time selling not drugs but religion. After hearing Malcolm's fiery speeches, the membership at the Harlem temple increased dramatically. By the end of the 1950s, thanks in large part to Malcolm's recruiting efforts, over fifty temples were in operation in the United States.

Journalist Keith A. Owens elaborates:

There is no question that the organization increased its numbers once he [Malcolm] was put in charge of growing the Nation, and at its peak, the Nation of Islam gained even a grudging respect from its detractors as the nation's only organization founded by blacks, run by blacks, funded by blacks, and therefore the only Black organization without any ties or obligations to any White groups.[27]

Owens is alluding to the fact that the National Association for the Advancement of Colored People (NAACP) had been organized by whites and was partially financed by white benefactors.

The White Man's Crimes

Throughout Malcolm's ministry with the Nation of Islam, many of his speeches and sermons focused on attacking the white man and his religion, Christianity. He often described how Christian missionaries converted many of their followers in Africa and elsewhere around the world, not with biblical teaching but with guns.

Malcolm believed wholeheartedly in the message of Elijah Muhammad that blacks would eventually overcome their second-class-citizenship position. "I have sat at the Messenger's feet, hearing the truth from his own mouth. I have pledged on my knees to Allah to tell the white man about his crimes and the black man the true teachings of our Honorable Elijah Muhammad."[28]

Whites called Malcolm a hatemonger. Goldman elaborates: "Malcolm . . . undertook to carry Harlem's fury downtown, to tell white people to their faces, in their own mass media, what ordinary blacks had been saying about them backstairs for all those years. Malcolm didn't teach hate, or need to; he exploited a vein that was already there."[29]

Essayist Cornel West agrees: "Malcolm X articulated Black rage in a manner unprecedented in American history. His style of communicating this rage bespoke a boiling urgency and an audacious sincerity: the substance of what he said highlighted the chronic refusal of most Americans to acknowledge the sheer absurdity that confronts human beings of African descent in this country."[30]

Malcolm X speaks at a rally in Harlem in 1963. During his speeches, Malcolm often condemned whites and the Christian religion.

Preaching and Ministering in Harlem

Malcolm was excited with the challenge of ministering in Harlem. All together, the area contained over a million black people, the largest concentrated population of blacks in the world. He was determined to reach as many of them as he could. He had various pamphlets printed detailing what the Nation of Islam was all about and scheduled meetings at various locations in the area. Then Malcolm went out to speak not only to groups but to anyone he passed on the streets who would listen.

Part of what made Malcolm X such an effective speaker was the skill that he had developed while in prison. Malcolm was a mesmerizing speaker who held his audience's attention and engaged their emotions. Journalist Peter Bailey elaborates: "I felt as if I was hearing the truth. I had never heard anyone speak with such clarity and forcefulness. And he just stimulated me."[31]

Malcolm's speaking style was praised by supporters and critics alike. He generally spoke in a conversational style while he addressed each individual personally. He spoke with intensity about the issues of the day and made blacks feel good about themselves. He did this by using highly emotional appeals to the masses, using street words with the same eloquence he devoted to more conventional phrases. He also earned their respect because he had rid himself of all the ills that most affected the masses: drugs, alcohol, and criminal actions.

In many ways, Malcolm became the voice of the Nation of Islam. Cone elaborates: "Malcolm was committed to telling the truth as he felt it and with the simplicity, clarity, and passion of an angry biblical prophet."[32]

Condemnation of the Civil Rights Movement

Malcolm's speeches continued to draw hundreds of new members. The majority of these new recruits were young black men who agreed that the nonviolent approach of other black leaders was not producing results in the civil rights movement.

The rapid growth of the Nation of Islam coincided with the growth of the civil rights movement in America. The civil rights movement had begun in December 1955 when seamstress Rosa Parks was arrested in Montgomery, Alabama, for refusing to give up her seat on a bus. Her action motivated other African Americans in

Montgomery, led by the charismatic Baptist minister Martin Luther King Jr., to launch a bus boycott. Meeting with success in Alabama, King and others expanded the movement to address discrimination issues throughout the South and elsewhere.

Malcolm X and the Nation of Islam believed that the leaders of the civil rights movement were trying to achieve equality the wrong way. The organization that was at the forefront of the civil rights movement was the National Association for the Advancement of Colored People. Formed in 1909, the organization worked to bring about the end of segregation by challenging it legally. To accomplish this, King and other black leaders advocated a nonviolent approach to achieving equality and integration. Malcolm, on the other hand, believed that blacks, frequently

Civil rights leader Martin Luther King Jr. delivers his "I Have a Dream" speech in 1963. Malcolm X and the members of the Nation of Islam repeatedly criticized King's nonviolent approach to achieving equality and integration.

the victims of white violence, should not rely on nonviolent methods to achieve their goals.

Malcolm repeatedly criticized King's approach and called for blacks to create their own society. Malcolm's ultimate goal was the liberation of blacks from what he believed to be a violent, oppressive white-dominated society. While King wanted blacks to fit into the present society, Malcolm wanted the destruction of this system. He wanted it replaced with a system and government that allowed blacks and whites to share power equally. Malcolm spoke: "We are not fighting for integration. . . . We are fighting for recognition as human beings."[33]

Malcolm Earns Respect

Malcolm's message resonated with blacks throughout the country, especially those who lived in northern ghettos. Because of their poverty and oppression, African Americans in the ghettos found hope and encouragement in Malcolm's words. While his words had brought Malcolm recognition, an incident that occurred in Harlem would turn that recognition into respect.

This incident occurred in April 1958 and showed the power that Malcolm X had over his followers. It began with the arrest and beating of a black man named Johnson Hinton. Hinton had spoken out about a black beating and had then been beaten himself. Bleeding, Hinton was dragged to jail even though he had not committed a crime.

Malcolm and a large contingent of the Fruit of Islam (a paramilitary group of Muslim men in the Nation of Islam) responded. They marched in formation to the police station where Hinton was imprisoned. The group soon swelled to more than eight hundred people.

Malcolm X entered the police station alone, demanding to see the prisoner. In a firm and steady voice, he informed the police authorities that the large crowd of black men would remain outside the station until Hinton received medical attention. Fearing violence, the police acquiesced.

Cone describes what happened next: "After the police gave him their promise . . . Malcolm did something that stunned the police and established him as a leader in the black community who must be reckoned with. He strode to the head of the angry,

Marriage

In the midst of his recruiting and speeches, Malcolm X found someone who shared his beliefs and could share his life. Her name was Sister Betty X. After graduating from high school, Betty attended Tuskegee Institute in Alabama, one of the first black schools dedicated to preparing black students for work in various vocations. She then moved to New York City, where she obtained her nursing diploma from Brooklyn State Hospital.

While Betty was at school in New York, a friend took her to hear Malcolm X speak. Betty was immediately impressed with the tall minister who spoke of the evils of segregation. Betty stated: "Well, he got to the podium—and I sat up straight. I was impressed with him." The two were introduced and saw each other frequently after Betty joined the Harlem temple, where she began to teach hygiene and other health issues to young Muslim girls and women.

Malcolm found Sister Betty an avid supporter of the Black Muslim faith and was attracted to her. They never dated as such, because their religion encouraged single men and women to go out in large groups. Despite this and Malcolm's hectic schedule, the connection between the two strengthened. Eventually, Malcolm called her on the telephone and proposed. They were married less than a week later on January 14, 1958, before a justice of the peace. The couple eventually had four daughters.

Quoted in Gale Cengage Learning, "Betty Shabazz." www.gale.cengage.com/free_resources/blhm/ bio/ shabazz_b.htm.

Malcolm X poses with Qubilah (left) and Attallah (right), two of the four daughters he had with wife Betty.

impatient mob, stood silently, and then flicked his hands. Within seconds the street was empty."[34] This incident won great respect for Malcolm X and the Nation of Islam. New recruits came in at an even heightened pace.

A Wave of White Fear

While Malcolm X had gained quite a following in New York and elsewhere, he was still largely unknown to the American public. That would change in 1959. CBS Television newsman Mike Wallace, later a correspondent for *60 Minutes*, wanted to do a documentary on the Nation of Islam. Cameramen filmed in and around the temples in New York and elsewhere, while reporters interviewed both Elijah Muhammad and Malcolm X.

The television show, shown in the spring of 1959, provided the first glimpse that many Americans had of Malcolm X, Elijah Muhammad, and the Black Muslim movement. The documentary created a wave of fear among white viewers, who were bombarded with shocking images of thousands of blacks listening to the arousing words of Muslim speakers, notably Malcolm X. Cone elaborates: "White Americans saw and heard Malcolm X for the first time and were deeply shocked by what most of them believed was nothing but the preaching of black supremacy."[35]

Following the show there was an uproar from whites and a few

Malcolm X and the Black Muslim Movement were relatively unknown until television newsman Mike Wallace (pictured) did a documentary on Malcolm and the Nation of Islam in 1959.

blacks who believed that the Nation of Islam was encouraging violence. Elijah and Malcolm had been portrayed in the documentary as a sinister force that was extremely dangerous to the well-being of white Americans. Malcolm and his fiery words scared white television viewers; so much so that many began to view him as an evil hatemonger.

The television program made Malcolm X an instant star. His telephone began ringing off the hook as hundreds of reporters wanted an interview. His face began appearing on the covers of magazines as well, and journalists began labeling him "The New Black Voice."

The show also led to dozens of speaking engagements at college campuses throughout the United States. Malcolm felt exhilarated by the college students who asked probing questions and challenged him to be at his best. He told reporters that the students were generally objective in their opinions and searching for answers that he hoped to provide. Journalist Sulayman Nyang elaborates: "His speeches in colleges and universities and on television and radio galvanized a large number of young blacks in American ghettos."[36] While whites were shocked by the program, more than ten thousand blacks responded by joining the Nation of Islam.

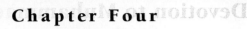

Chapter Four

A New Name— a New Outlook

After the 1959 CBS documentary on the Nation of Islam had aired, Malcolm continued his ministry. Malcolm, however, was becoming impatient with the failure of the Nation of Islam to become involved in the larger civil rights movement. Malcolm had gradually come to believe that the Nation of Islam should initiate more action-oriented programs coordinated with the King movement. He believed that militant Muslims should participate in the civil rights protests in the South and elsewhere. Muhammad did not agree.

Signs of other differences between the two men also began to appear more frequently in the early 1960s. As Malcolm's fame grew, Muhammad had grown concerned that Malcolm was in the limelight more often than he was. This did not sit well with the Nation's leader. Many others in the hierarchy of the Nation were also upset with Malcolm's popularity. Feelings of jealousy grew, especially after Malcolm was named as national minister in 1962.

By the early 1960s Malcolm X began hearing more and more negative remarks about himself from other members of the Nation of Islam. Malcolm, critics within the Nation claimed, was trying to take over the movement. He was accused of trying to build his own religious empire by taking credit for Muhammad's

Devotion to Muhammad

For the entire time that Malcolm was a member of the Nation of Islam, he considered Elijah Muhammad a father figure. His speeches were filled with Elijah's teachings. Many of the words he used were those Muhammad had taught him. Historian James H. Cone summarizes: "From the time of Malcolm X's sudden and radical conversion in 1948 . . . Malcolm's thinking was defined by his total commitment to Elijah Muhammad."[1] In fact, according to Malcolm's daughter Attallah: "If you quote him prior to 1962, you have to ask yourself if you're quoting Malcolm or the Nation because everything he said prior to 1962 came under the censorship of the (Nation's) Council."[2]

His devotion to Muhammad was absolute; he believed that Muhammad was divine. Many intimate associates claim that Muhammad loved Malcolm more than he did his own children, and Malcolm returned that love in kind. Malcolm stated in his autobiography: "I believed so strongly in Mr. Muhammad that I would have hurled myself between him and an assassin."[3]

Malcolm's attitude changed following his conflicts with the Nation of Islam. Muhammad, as well, began to severely criticize his former minister.

1. James H. Cone, *Martin and Malcolm and America: A Dream or a Nightmare*. Maryknoll, NY: Orbis, 1992, p. 92.

2. Quoted in Charles Whitaker, "Who Was Malcolm X?" *Ebony*, February 1, 1992.

3. Malcolm X with Alex Haley, *The Autobiography of Malcolm X*. New York: Grove, p. 290.

teachings. And yet in every speech Malcolm gave during this and earlier time periods, he prefaced his remarks with, "In the words of the Honorable Elijah Muhammad."

A Betrayal

Also around this time, Malcolm X learned some very disturbing news about Muhammad. Word leaked out that two paternity suits had been filed against the Nation's leader. Malcolm later told reporters that the Nation was trying to keep a scandal from developing over the pregnancy of one of Muhammad's secretaries.

At first Malcolm refused to believe the rumors that Muhammad could be guilty of adultery; adultery was strictly forbidden by their Islamic faith. The secretaries had been exiled from the Nation, but in order to determine the truth, Malcolm talked to them personally, despite a Muslim law that forbade contact with an exile. The women told him of their brief affairs with the Nation's leader; when word spread of their pregnancies, they were banned from the organization. Malcolm was devastated by this news. He considered Elijah Muhammad not only a father figure but a man who unquestionably followed the Muslim way of life.

Malcolm also talked to Muhammad's son Wallace, who confirmed that the accusations against his father were true. This confirmation troubled Malcolm, who feared that the Black Muslim movement could be irreparably damaged. He became even more concerned when he learned that many followers were leaving the Nation because of Muhammad's actions.

Malcolm flew to Arizona to meet with Muhammad in the spring of 1963. Muhammad admitted that the rumors were true. Malcolm later said that he felt betrayed by the man in whom he had placed so much love and trust. He compared his feelings to being a happily married person who suddenly finds out that his or her spouse wants a divorce. Malcolm told one reporter: "Every second of my twelve years with Mr. Muhammad, I had been ready to lay down my life for him. The thing to me worse than death was the betrayal."[37]

The Kennedy Comments

The relationship between Malcolm and Muhammad continued to deteriorate in early 1963. Then, in November 1963 President John F. Kennedy was assassinated in Dallas, Texas. When asked what he thought about the murder, Malcolm, without thinking, replied "that it was, as I saw it, a case of the chickens coming home to roost."[38] He later explained that he was insinuating that the white man's hatred had not stopped with the killing of blacks but had ascended to the presidency of the United States.

People across the nation were outraged by his remarks, which were understood to mean that Malcolm was glad that Kennedy had been killed. Malcolm was immediately criticized for his remarks by the Nation of Islam. He was called before Muhammad and told that his remarks made all Muslims look bad. As a result of his comment, Malcolm was told that he would have to refrain

During a speech after the 1963 assassination of President John F. Kennedy, Malcolm X made controversial remarks regarding the murder, for which he was punished by Elijah Muhammad.

from making any public comments for the next ninety days. Many historians believe that the punishment derived not so much from the comments about Kennedy as from the fact that Malcolm had discovered the truth about Muhammad's private life.

Malcolm X was astonished by the harsh punishment; he was told that he could not sermonize or speak out to any audience for three months. He felt he was being disciplined for simply speaking his own mind. No punishment could have been worse for Malcolm, yet despite his shock he agreed to abide by the order.

Not long after the punishment began, Malcolm began to hear the first of numerous death threats from members of the Nation of Islam, who believed Malcolm had betrayed the organization by challenging Muhammad's ethics. His temporary exile from the Nation also led to increasing talk about Malcolm trying to take over the organization and replace Muhammad as the new leader. More rumors followed that higher authorities in the Nation were preparing to oust Malcolm. Goldman summarizes: "For the Nation, Malcolm was both competitor and blasphemer—a heretic who had slandered God by questioning the morality and authority of His Last Messenger."[39]

When the ninety days were over, Muhammad extended the punishment for an indefinite time without giving Malcolm any coherent reason for this action. Malcolm felt even more devastated and reluctantly decided to leave the Nation of Islam and create a new organization. In March 1964 Malcolm announced that he was leaving. When he had joined the organization it had less than four hundred members; when he left it had forty thousand. He was thirty-eight years old.

Muslim Mosque, Inc.

Following his split with the Nation of Islam, Malcolm X announced the formation on March 12, 1964, of a new mosque, calling it the Muslim Mosque, Inc. He appealed to blacks of all religions to join, hoping that this new organization would provide a solid religious base for the members of Harlem's ghettos. Malcolm stated that the Muslim Mosque would be similar to the Nation of Islam's but that he would not be worshipped as a god like Muhammad was. He told his followers that he was a simple preacher, not a prophet.

In forming this group, Malcolm stated: "I feel like a man who has been asleep somewhat and under someone else's control. I feel what I'm thinking and saying now is for myself. Before it was for and by guidance of another [Muhammad], now I think with my own mind."[40] While Malcolm readily admitted that the Nation of Islam and Elijah Muhammad had helped him gain self-respect, he also stated that the organization had censored many of his comments and stances. He was now able to speak freely about the issues that meant the most to him.

The new mosque, however, was poorly attended from the beginning. Malcolm had hoped that others within the Nation of Islam would follow him, but he was disillusioned when most preferred to stay with the Nation.

A Journey to the Holy Land

Following his departure from the Nation of Islam, Malcolm X became more interested in traditional Islam. In 1964 he began meeting with Mahmoud Youssef Shawarbi, an Egyptian who led the Islamic Center in New York City. Shawarbi taught Malcolm about the traditional Islamic religion as practiced by Muslims throughout the world.

Partly as a result of these lessons, Malcolm decided to make a hajj, or pilgrimage, to Mecca in Saudi Arabia. A holy journey there was not required by the Nation of Islam but was part of the traditional Islamic religious requirements. In Islamic law, making the hajj means journeying to the Kaaba, the Sacred House, as well as fulfilling other pilgrimage rites.

Malcolm left on April 13, 1964, flying from New York City to Frankfurt, Germany, and from there to Cairo, Egypt. In Cairo he joined a group of Muslim pilgrims making the holy journey to Mecca. Initially, he felt out of place since he did not know the traditional prayers or customs, but he learned quickly and soon felt part of the group.

He, like the rest of the group, donned the traditional clothes worn for the pilgrimage, a set of white cloths, one worn over the shoulder, the other around the waist. One cloth, the *izar,* was folded around his hips, while the other, the *rida,* was worn on his upper body, draped around his neck and left arm. His right arm was kept bare. He carried a money belt and also a bag that held

After Malcolm X left the Nation of Islam, he became interested in traditional Islam. In April 1964 he flew to Saudi Arabia on a pilgrimage to the holy city of Mecca, where he met with Prince Faisal al-Saud.

his passport and other papers. To complete the outfit, Malcolm donned a pair of sandals, called the *na'l*. Every one of the thousands of pilgrims at the Cairo airport was wearing the same outfit as they boarded planes to take them to Jedda in Saudi Arabia. Malcolm was astounded that even the most important officials wore the same clothing as the poorest peasant.

Completing the Hajj

Once they arrived in Saudi Arabia, Malcolm and his fellow travelers were assigned a guide named Mutawaf, who would be responsible for getting the party from Jedda to Mecca. Jedda, a city on the Red Sea, was the arrival and disembarkation point for all pilgrims. It was located about 40 miles [64km] from Mecca.

Their first stop was the Kaaba, located in the courtyard of the Great Mosque. The Kaaba is a small building that contains a sacred black stone. For Muslims, the holiest building is the Great Mosque, and the most important symbol is the Kaaba. After repeated prayer, Malcolm, as a pilgrim, kissed the Kaaba. After circling the Kaaba a number of times, the pilgrims then headed toward Mount Arafat. Mount Arafat, known also as the Mountain of Mercy, is the site where the Prophet Muhammad delivered his farewell sermon hundreds of years earlier. Failure to ascend the mountain negates the pilgrimage. They arrived at the mountaintop at noon and spent the afternoon praying. They departed at sunset, their pigrimage completed.

A New Name—a New Outlook

While in the Middle East, Malcolm's feelings about the white man began to undergo a significant change. As Malcolm had watched the various pilgrims board the plane to Mecca, he was hit by the absence of color or prestige problems. "You could be a king or a peasant and no one would know. . . . Packed in the plane were white, black, brown, red, and yellow people, blue eyes and blond hair, and my kinky red hair—all together, brothers! All honoring the same God Allah, all in turn giving honor to each other."[41]

Malcolm was determined upon returning to the United States that the American public understand the Islamic faith because of its tolerance for all races. To accomplish this, he wrote letters to his family and colleagues in America and also wrote an open letter to the press. In a letter to his associates at the Muslim Mosque, Malcolm wrote: "Never have I witnessed such sincere hospitality and the overwhelming spirit of true brotherhood as is practiced by people of all colors and races here in this Ancient Holy Land. . . . For the past week, I have been utterly speechless and spellbound by the graciousness I see displayed all around me by people of all colors."[42] He continued: "During the past eleven days

After returning from the Middle East, Malcolm X was determined to help the American public embrace tolerance for all races, a major teaching of traditional Islam.

here in the Muslim world, I have eaten from the same plate, drank from the same glass, and slept in the same bed . . . while praying to the same God—with fellow Muslims, whose eyes were the bluest of blue, whose hair was the blondest of blond, and whose skin was the whitest of white."[43]

Malcolm also took a new name, El-Hajj Malik el-Shabazz. The Shabazz were a tribe of black people who had migrated from East Asia to Africa more than fifty thousand years ago. "El-Hajj" meant that he had undertaken the pilgrimage; "Malik" was the Arabic version of Malcolm.

White reporters could hardly believe this was the same man who had preached a doctrine of hatred and violence. Journalist Margaret Snyder, for instance, had met Malcolm while he was still a member of the Nation of Islam. She met him again in Mecca after his pilgrimage. She wrote about the huge difference she saw in the black leader: "I could see no trace of racism remaining in Malcolm X. The impact of Mecca . . . enhanced by his unique ability to assimilate ideas and viewpoints, was profound."[44]

Spiritual Rebirth

After also meeting with various African leaders to earn their support for his projects and to offer his assistance with their movements, Malcolm returned to New York on May 21, 1964. He had gone to Africa to find his true religion; he had found much more. He had learned that his earlier beliefs about race were false. When he spoke to the media upon his arrival in New York, he told the press that he no longer believed that all whites were devils. He told everyone he talked to that he had undergone a spiritual rebirth.

He had also discovered that a good part of the world saw him as one of the leaders of America's black population. Malcolm returned, determined to finish his autobiography, which he had begun working on a couple of years earlier, and also to work toward an international approach to black freedom. Malcolm explained: "When humanity looks upon itself not as black men, white men, brown men, red men, and yellow men, but as human beings, then they will sit down together in peace. . . . The only time you'll have a society on this earth when all men will live as brothers will be when all respect each other and treat each other as brothers."[45]

Meeting with African Leaders

After his pilgrimage to Mecca, Malcolm met with Prince Faisal, the ruler of Saudi Arabia. Malcolm was treated like a head of state, and the two leaders spent many hours talking about the black man's plight in the United States.

Wherever he went, in fact, Malcolm was treated like royalty. He also visited Lebanon in the Middle East; Morocco and Algeria in North Africa; and Nigeria, Ghana, and Senegal in West Africa. With all the leaders he met, Malcolm discussed his plans to link African Americans with blacks from all over the world. He believed that all people of African descent should be working together to improve the black way of life for everyone. He was convinced that the black freedom movement in America should not be separated from the liberation struggles that were occurring in many African countries.

Malcolm believed that the majority of major American black groups were making a mistake by not communicating with the independent nations of Africa and their black leaders. He hoped to remedy this neglect with the formation of the Organization of Afro-American Unity.

The Organization of Afro-American Unity

Many historians agree that the one quality Malcolm showed throughout his life was the ability to change. This was particularly apparent after his visit to Mecca. Cone concludes: "He was a complex person—constantly growing, disavowing old views and affirming new ones."[46] Malcolm himself explained the changes: "My pilgrimage broadened my scope. It blessed me with new insight."[47]

As part of this new international outlook, Malcolm founded the Organization of Afro-American Unity. He copied many of the ideas for this organization from the Organization of African Unity, a group that included representatives from all the independent African nations who were ridding themselves of colonialism and oppression.

In his autobiography Malcolm X explains why he wanted to create a new organization:

I felt a challenge to plan, and build, an organization that could help cure the black man in North America of the sickness which had kept [him] under the white man's heel. . . . Twenty-two million black men! They have given America four hundred years of toil; they have bled and died in every battle since the Revolution; they were in America before the Pilgrims, and long before the mass immigrations —and they are still today at the bottom of everything![48]

Malcolm X gives his first public address on behalf of his newly founded Organization of Afro-American Unity on June 28, 1964.

On June 28, 1964, he made his first public address on behalf of this new organization at the Audubon Ballroom in Harlem. He stated:

> I have realized . . . that our African brothers have gained their independence faster than you and I here in America have. . . . Just ten years ago on the African continent, our people were colonized . . . and in a short time, they have gained more independence, more recognition, more respect as human beings than you and I have. And you and I live in a country which is supposed to be the citadel of education, freedom, justice, democracy. . . .
>
> [The aim of this new organization is] to fight whoever gets in our way, to bring about the complete independence of people of African descent here in the Western Hemisphere.[49]

His long-term goal was to unite all blacks, in the United States and abroad, into one united force to fight for freedom from oppression and discrimination.

Malcolm also began appealing to other revolutionary groups throughout the world. Editor Steve Clark elaborates: "[He] began to explain, and act on, the need for Black organizations to forge alliances—as equals—with other groups of working people and youth who had proven themselves in practice to be committed to revolutionary change by any means necessary."[50]

Black Pride

Malcolm X, in announcing the formation of the Organization of Afro-American Unity, stated firmly that it was the absolute right of all African Americans to control their own destiny. He advocated black control of every aspect of the black community. West elaborates: "Malcolm X's notion . . . holds that Black people must no longer view themselves through white lenses. His claim is that Black people will never value themselves as long as they subscribe to a standard that devalues them."[51]

Furthermore, Malcolm X spoke of the need for the black community to help each other in every way possible. He said, "As other ethnic groups have done, let the black people, wherever

After founding the Organization of Afro-American Unity in 1964,
Malcolm X (right) agreed to work with Martin Luther King Jr. (left)
to help African Americans in their struggle for civil rights.

possible, however possible, patronize their own kind, hire their own kind, and start in those ways to build up the black race's ability to do for itself. That's the only way the American black man is ever going to get respect."[52] He then added: "A race of people is like an individual man; until it uses its own talent, takes pride in its own history, expresses its own culture, affirms its own selfhood, it can never fulfill itself."[53]

Malcolm also spoke of the need for African Americans to be proud of being black. He stated: "We have been a people who hated all our African characteristics. We hated our hair, we hated

Changing His View on Civil Rights

Prior to his trip to Mecca, Malcolm had avoided any direct involvement in the civil rights movement, mainly at the request of the Nation of Islam. But when Malcolm formed the Organization of Afro-American Unity, he announced plans to join with other civil rights leaders in bringing about change. He stated:

> I am not out to fight other Negro leaders or organizations. We must find a common approach, a common solution, to a common problem. . . . It's time for us to submerge our differences and realize that . . . we have the same problem. . . . Whether you're educated or illiterate, whether you live on the boulevard or in the alley, [the result of being black is the same.] They don't hang you because you're a Baptist, they hang you because you're black.

While Malcolm had previously concentrated all his efforts on helping northern blacks, he decided in February 1965 to work in Selma, Alabama. He announced he would take part in a rally there for voting rights. Civil rights leader Martin Luther King Jr. was already in Selma and had, in fact, been jailed. King's supporters, including his wife, Coretta, feared that Malcolm's appearance and words might incite the crowd to violence. Malcolm surprised them, however, by speaking calmly and calling for King's release. With Malcolm's participation in Selma, King and other black leaders hoped that an alliance could indeed be formed between the two leaders.

Quoted in James H. Cone, *Martin and Malcolm and America: A Dream or a Nightmare.* Maryknoll, NY: Orbis, 1992, p. 193.

the shape of our nose . . . hated the blood of Africa that was in our veins. And in hating our features and our skin and our blood, we had to end up hating ourselves."[54] As part of this pride, Malcolm X told his followers that the use of the word "negro" was demeaning; he believed that the terms "Afro-American," "African," and "Black" were more fitting for the image he wanted to create.

He envisioned the Organization of Afro-American Unity as a way of reeducating the black public. He stressed, in particular, the importance of education for all African Americans, stating: "Education is an important element in the struggle for human rights. It is the means to help our children and our people rediscover their identity and thereby increase their self-respect."[55] Malcolm X saw a need for more black teachers and principals as well as a need for textbooks to be changed to include a more accurate presentation of black history.

To achieve these goals and to obtain equality, Malcolm stressed that blacks must first attain human rights. "It is not integration that Negroes in America want, it is human dignity," he contended. "They want to be recognized as human beings. We are fighting for the right to live as free humans in this society. . . . We must have human rights before we can secure civil rights. We must be respected as human beings before we can be recognized as citizens."[56]

Malcolm also announced that he was ready to work with Martin Luther King Jr. and other civil rights leaders to achieve these rights. Civil rights leaders in the South were undertaking a massive voting drive, determined to register as many blacks as possible to vote in upcoming elections.

"By Any Means Necessary"

He was not ready, however, to agree with King about nonviolence. Malcolm frequently asserted the black right to self-defense. He stated: "Since self-preservation is the first law of nature, we assert the Afro-American's right to self-defense. We assert that in those areas where the government is either unable or unwilling to protect the lives and property of our people, that our people are within our rights to protect themselves by whatever means necessary."[57] Malcolm concluded: "By any means necessary . . . including violent means."[58]

The term "by any means necessary" drew criticism from whites across the country. Malcolm's response to the criticism was simple: "Not a single white person in America would sit idly by and let someone do to him what we blacks have been letting others do to us."[59] He argued that extremism was not a radical move but a logical one in responding to the failure of the government to end segregation. In his autobiography, Malcolm wrote: "I am for violence if non-violence means we continue postponing a solution to the American black man's problem—just to avoid violence."[60] At the time Malcolm made these comments, conditions had not significantly improved for black Americans. While some desegregation in southern schools had occurred, the pace was slow, and in many areas blacks were still being discriminated against. Despite laws that enabled blacks to vote, few were being allowed to do so. Change was coming, but far too slowly for Malcolm's liking. African Americans were still being treated as second-class citizens, having few of the things that whites took for granted, like good schools, comfortable homes, and decent salaries.

"Indict Uncle Sam"

As part of his new international outlook, Malcolm also decided to bring African American grievances before the United Nations. He announced that his new organization would

> work with every leader and . . . organization in this country interested in a program designed to bring your and my problem before the United Nations. . . . We feel that the problem of the black man in this country is beyond the ability of the United States government to solve. . . . So we must take it out of the hands of the United States government. And the only way to do this is by internationalizing it and taking advantage of the United Nations Declaration of Human Rights . . . where we can indict Uncle Sam for the continued criminal injustices that our people experience.[61]

Malcolm believed that the United States government had failed for too many years to resolve the problem of segregation and racism. He stated: "It makes America look ridiculous to stand up in world conferences and refer to herself as the leader of the

A crowd gathers to listen to Malcolm X speak about his decision to bring the issue of injustice against African Americans before the United Nations.

free world. Here is a country . . . standing up and pointing a finger [at others] . . . and there are twenty million black people in this country who are still confined to second-class citizenship, twenty million people in this country who are still segregated."[62]

Malcolm was determined to explore every avenue in order to improve the situation for African Americans in the United States.

Chapter Five

The Death and Legacy of Malcolm X

Malcolm X's agenda for the Organization of Afro-American Unity was specific and ambitious and brought praise from many blacks and whites alike. Events had already been set in motion, however, that would prevent him from ever seeing his dreams come to fruition.

Growing Death Threats

At the time, the Cold War between the United States and the Soviet Union had been heating up. The director of the Federal Bureau of Investigation (FBI), J. Edgar Hoover, suspected all of the civil rights leaders, including Malcolm X and Martin Luther King Jr., of Communist leanings and believed they posed a danger to the country. In addition, the FBI and government leaders were concerned about the threat of revolution if black leaders were to encourage their followers to rebel. As a result, wiretaps on the phones of many black leaders were approved and black federal agents were encouraged to infiltrate many civil rights organizations.

As early as March 1964, the FBI had recorded a telephone call from Elijah Muhammad to Minister Louis X (Louis Farrakhan) of Boston. In this call, according to biographer and author Karl Evanzz, "Muhammad said that Malcolm had to be silenced before he revealed too many scandalous secrets."[63] Several months later, in September, Muhammad gathered a select group of followers and spoke to them for over seven hours. The FBI reports: "He said that Malcolm X Little was the greatest hypocrite and must be stopped at all costs. Other hypocrites were to be taken care of, either by beatings or killings."[64]

In late 1964 the beatings began when several of Malcolm's aides were attacked by members of the Nation of Islam. Then in December Malcolm himself began to receive almost daily death

Louis Farrakhan

Louis Farrakhan, born Louis Eugene Walcott in 1933, in his early life had been a noted musician, singing, dancing, and playing the violin. He eventually gave up show business, took the name Louis X in July 1955, and became a minister at the Nation of Islam's Boston Temple.

After Malcolm's death, Farrakhan became the head of the Harlem Mosque and became the Nation's number one spokesman. Following Muhammad's death, he and Elijah's son Wallace (Warith Deen Muhammad) differed in their beliefs about the future of the Nation of Islam. Wallace distanced himself from some of the mystical origins of the Nation and changed the name to the Muslim American Society. Eventually Farrakhan reestablished the Nation of Islam, assumed the leadership of the organization, and has been its primary spokesman for over thirty years. Under his leadership the Black Muslims have thrived and grown in membership.

In 1995 he organized the Million Man March in Washington, D.C. Nearly 2 million black men attended the successful march and vowed to renew their commitment to African American growth. Another march called the Million More Movement occurred in October 2005 and stressed the continuing needs of black Americans. Farrakhan has been denounced by many black leaders for his continued doctrine of hatred against the white man and has also been heavily criticized for his anti-Semitic remarks.

Malcolm X's home was firebombed during the night of February 14, 1965. He is seen here on the following morning as he arrives to assess the damage.

threats. He spoke of these threats in his autobiography: "The first direct order for my death was issued through a Mosque Seven [Harlem] official who previously had been a close assistant. Another previously close assistant of mine was assigned to do the job. He was a brother with a knowledge of demolition; he was asked to wire my car to explode when I turned the ignition key. But this brother . . . instead . . . came to me."[65]

Several other attempts were made on Malcolm's life in early 1965. In Chicago he was ambushed by two men who pulled their car alongside his vehicle. Malcolm responded by sticking a cane out the window. Thinking it was a weapon, the other car sped away. And while on a trip to France, he received a number of other death threats. The French government, stating it did not want the burden of publicity that would follow any incident, asked Malcolm X to leave the country. In all, he barely escaped assassination attempts in France, Boston, New York, Chicago, and Los Angeles.

After leaving France, he returned to New York on February 13, 1965. Malcolm and his family were awakened in the middle of the following night by an explosion. Their house in Queens had been firebombed. Malcolm gathered up his children and made sure everyone got out of the house safely. More than 50 percent of the home was destroyed. He refused the offers of several friends to house him and his family, stating that he was afraid he would put them in danger.

Goldman summarizes:

> At the end, death was closing on him, and everybody saw it. . . . His friends saw it: they begged him to get out of town for a while—to Africa, to Europe, to California, anywhere away from Harlem and the most visible of his enemies. And Malcolm X saw it. He told people that he didn't care really, not for himself, but he lived out his last weeks and months jumping at street sounds and flinching at shadows.[66]

Shortly before he died, Malcolm stated: "I know that societies often have killed the people who have helped to change those societies. And if I can die having brought any light, having exposed any meaningful truth that will help destroy the racist cancer that is malignant in the body of America—then, all of the credit is due to Allah. Only the mistakes have been mine."[67]

Assassination

Despite the death threats, Malcolm X continued to speak out. At an engagement in Selma, Alabama, he spoke to the Student Non-violent Coordinating Committee about the racial injustices still evident in the South. He then returned to New York in order to speak at the Audubon Ballroom in Harlem on Sunday, February 21, 1965. More than four hundred wooden chairs had been set up in the ballroom so his supporters could hear him speak. Malcolm invited his wife, Betty Shabazz, who was pregnant, and his daughters to attend and hear his speech.

Security that day was unusually light. Malcolm, for instance, had requested that body searches at the door be eliminated because of the discomfort to supporters. In addition, the New York City police who were supposed to be stationed outside had been cancelled by someone allegedly calling on Malcolm's behalf. Goldman elaborates: "Malcolm had begun worrying that the talk of death and the martial aura of policemen and armed guards and body searches were frightening people away from the meetings. But the result was to lay him wide open to the men who had been hunting him."[68]

After driving himself to the ballroom, Malcolm waited offstage while listening to several other speakers. Then he appeared onstage, wearing a dark suit, white shirt, and thin tie, and strode to the dais, planning to talk about the foolishness of black men fighting other black men. After being introduced, he spoke his traditional greeting: "As Salaam Alaikum" or "peace be with you." The audience's response was: "Wa-alaikum salaam," or "unto you be peace."

Before Malcolm could begin his speech, however, a commotion broke out in the audience; a smoke bomb went off. His bodyguards left the front of the auditorium to settle the commotion, leaving Malcolm open and unguarded. During the confusion, a man sitting in the front row took out a sawed-off shotgun and fired at Malcolm. Two other men with handguns raced forward, also shooting at the black leader. Malcolm X was struck by sixteen bullets and fell backward. One woman sitting near the front described what she saw: "The commotion . . . diverted me just for an instant, then I turned back to look at Malcolm X just

Malcolm X is wheeled away on a stretcher after being shot during a rally at the Audubon Ballroom in Harlem, New York, on February 21, 1965. He died a short time later.

in time to see at least three men in the front row stand and take aim and start firing simultaneously. It looked like a firing squad."[69]

Chaos erupted in the ballroom as audience members dived for safety. Betty Shabazz, after making sure her children were safe, rushed onto the stage to comfort her husband. In the meantime, someone ran across the street to the Columbia-Presbyterian Hospital, obtained a stretcher, and took Malcolm to the hospital. Doctors opened his chest in an attempt to resuscitate him but were unsuccessful; he was pronounced dead at 3:15 in the afternoon. Within minutes, the news was spreading across Harlem and then New York City. Friedly summarizes: "Malcolm X's bold prediction of a violent death finally came to fruition three months before his fortieth birthday."[70]

His assailants fled immediately after the shooting. One of them, Talmadge Hayer, was chased by an armed member of Malcolm's security force. Hayer was shot in the leg and collapsed on the sidewalk, where he was pummeled by angry spectators. Two patrolling policemen arrived on the scene and arrested Hayer.

Trying to put together what had actually happened was a difficult job for the investigating officers. No two spectators had seen the same thing. Despite the conflicting stories, the police were able to arrest two more men, Norman 3X Butler and Thomas 15X Johnson, a few weeks later. Hayer denied being Muslim and claimed that he had been paid to kill the black leader; the other two assassins were members of the Nation of Islam, although Hayer loudly proclaimed their innocence. Reports that two other people had been involved in creating diversions such as the smoke bomb were investigated, but no other arrests were made.

Eulogies and Condemnations

Malcolm X's funeral was held on February 27, 1965, at Faith Temple Church of God in Harlem. Betty had difficulty finding a place to hold her husband's funeral because of the potential for violence. Bishop Alvin Childs of the Faith Temple eventually agreed to have the service at his church, a former movie theater that held more than one thousand people. Despite bomb threats that closed the church for brief periods during the four days it was open for mourners to view his casket, seventeen hundred mourners filled the church for the funeral, while over six thousand more people waited in the streets outside the temple, straining to hear the eulogies.

Time magazine describes the funeral: "He [Malcolm X] wore the white robe that signified his faith. In the four days before his burial, more than 20,000 persons, almost all Negroes, filed past his body as it lay on view in a glass-topped, wrought-copper casket. Following Muslim custom, when Malcolm was buried . . . his head was to the east, toward Mecca."[71] Prior to being placed in the casket, his body had been prepared according to Muslim traditions. Malcolm was bathed in holy oils and draped in seven white linen shrouds so that only his face could be seen.

One of the most moving eulogies at the funeral was given by black activist and award-winning actor Ossie Davis. A longtime friend of Malcolm's, he spoke of Malcolm being a hero to blacks across the world. He stated:

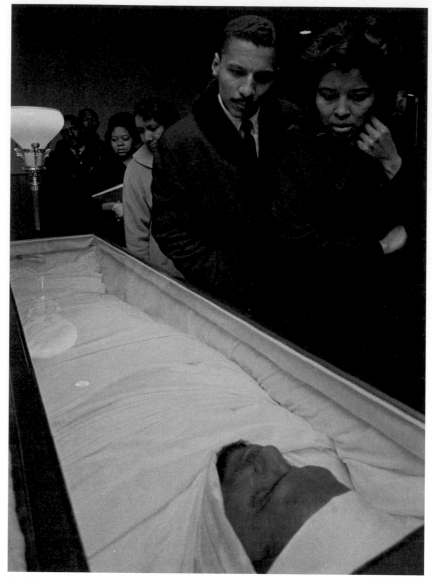

In February 1965 mourners pay their respects to Malcolm X, whose body is wrapped in seven white linen shrouds in accordance with Islamic tradition.

Here—at this final hour, in this quiet place—Harlem has come to bid farewell to one of its brightest hopes. . . . For Harlem is where he worked and where he struggled and fought. . . .

Nobody knew better than he the power words had over minds of men. Malcolm had stopped being a Negro years ago. It had become too small, too puny, too weak a word for him. Malcolm was bigger than that. Malcolm had become an Afro-American. . . .

There are those who will consider it their duty . . . to tell us to revile him, to flee, even from the presence of his memory, to save ourselves by writing him out of the history of our turbulent times. . . . They will say he is of hate—a fanatic, a racist—who can only bring evil to the cause for which you struggle. And we will answer and say to them: Did you ever talk to Brother Malcolm? Did you ever touch him or have him smile at you? Did you ever really listen to him?

Malcolm was our manhood, our living, black manhood . . . and in honoring him, we honor the best in ourselves. . . .

Our shining Prince! Who didn't hesitate to die, because he loved us so.[72]

While thousands of his supporters and friends praised Malcolm for his courage and commitment to the black community, many others were critical. Many newspaper editorials condemned Malcolm for his "doctrine of hatred," while some even hinted that Malcolm had gotten what he deserved.

Elijah Muhammad, who had once thought of Malcolm as a son, called him a hypocrite and said "that Malcolm X got just what he preached."[73] Muhammad went on to remark that the Nation of Islam could not tolerate such a man of violence because their organization advocated peace.

A *Time* magazine editorial on March 5, 1965, also condemned and criticized Malcolm X. "Malcolm X had been a pimp, a cocaine addict, and a thief. . . . His gospel was hatred. . . . His creed was violence. . . . Yet even before his bullet-ridden body went to its grave, Malcolm X was being sanctified. Negro leaders called him brilliant. . . . In fact, Malcolm X—in life and in death—was a disaster to the civil rights movement."[74] *Time* magazine, along with the *New York Times* and other major newspapers, had been among the harshest and most outspoken critics of Malcolm X during his lifetime.

Assassination Theories

The three men who were arrested following Malcolm's assassination were tried, found guilty, and sentenced to prison terms. Hayer, the man wounded at the scene, admitted that he was paid for the crime but did not identify the source until after Elijah Muhammad's death in 1975. At that time, Hayer admitted that the Nation of Islam had been responsible. He told officials that he had been recruited by two members of the Nation's Newark, New Jersey, mosque. He also insisted that members of that mosque had been involved in the actual shooting and that Johnson and Butler had had nothing to do with the crime. From whom the orders came has never been fully determined. Johnson, one of the imprisoned men, later stated: "Malcolm X was a dead man the minute he told the media about Honorable Elijah Muhammad's personal life. From that day forward it was just a matter of time."[75]

Farrakhan, the current leader of the Nation of Islam, publicly acknowledged during a 2000 *60 Minutes* interview that he and the Nation were guilty of at least complicity in the assassination. He had admitted even earlier, in 1991, that he himself had helped

In 2000 Nation of Islam leader Louis Farrakhan (left) acknowledged that he and the Nation helped create the hatred toward Malcolm X that led to his assassination.

create the climate of hatred toward Malcolm that led to the murder. In a speech given on February 21, 1993, Farrakhan told the audience: "When Malcolm leveled attacks against Nation of Islam founder Elijah Muhammad, he stepped across a line that made death inevitable."[76]

Despite the inevitability of Malcolm's death, Farrakhan continues to deny charges that someone in the Nation of Islam actually ordered or paid for the assassination. Most of Malcolm's supporters and many historians disagree. Friedly summarizes: "Malcolm X represented the greatest threat to the Nation of Islam that it had faced since the inception of the movement in the 1930s. Its former minister had the potential to draw large numbers of the Islamic faithful into his organization."[77]

All three men imprisoned for the assassination have been released from prison, and all have given press interviews. In fact, one of them, Norman 3X Butler, was appointed to head the same Harlem mosque where Malcolm had preached. No one has implicated Elijah Muhammad or Louis Farrakhan in the planning or the execution of the murder. Notes writer Karl Evanzz, "No specific order was necessary, they say. Once Malcolm . . . had been denounced as a 'devil,' a traitor to the Nation of Islam, they say it was their duty to take appropriate action."[78]

Many other individuals and groups, however, claim that Malcolm's death was the result of a conspiracy. While most point to the Nation of Islam, many others contend that the U.S. government in the form of the Central Intelligence Agency (CIA) or the FBI was involved. Some have even mentioned that the New York City Police Department was part of the conspiracy. Even the drug cartels and drug lords of New York were suspected. Friedly elaborates: "Malcolm's leftward [toward communism] leanings were the background to the government's motive for killing him. . . . It was [Malcolm's] attempt to bring the United States before the United Nations to face charges of racism that provided the impetus for the murder."[79] The controversies and theories continue to this day.

The "What Ifs"

In the years following his death, Malcolm's image and the importance of his words and actions began to take on immense overtones. He was elevated to the position of a martyr and saint.

Goldman elaborates:

> And now we have the Malcolm legend, the man layered over by the myth.
>
> . . .We have a Malcolm who was about to announce a program that would surely have achieved the liberation of the blacks; who had successfully begun building a revolutionary mass organization of the ghetto street people; who would shortly have converged with Martin Luther King Jr. in a mighty alliance of the black and maybe all the oppressed against poverty, racism, and war . . . who was at the very eve of bringing the United States into the dock at the United Nations and exposing its hypocrisies to the world.[80]

Malcolm's death prevented the world from ever finding out if his ambitious program would have come to fruition or exactly what his future contributions to the civil rights movement would have been. But the guessing and the "what ifs" have continued. The largest area of speculation has surrounded the possibility that Malcolm would have allied himself with King. What would the two men have done if they had worked together—or lived longer? Cone voices his opinion: "Despite the optimistic forecasts . . . it was not likely that Martin's white benefactors would have allowed public cooperation between him and Malcolm to take place. . . . For white liberals Malcolm was too unpredictable and thus not subject to their control."[81]

The Autobiography of Malcolm X

Prior to his death, Malcolm had spent many months (1963–1965) with author Alex Haley, working on an autobiography. Haley completed the book following the assassination and began the process of finding a publisher. He met with difficulties but finally persuaded Grove Press, a company known for defying restrictions against publishing controversial books, to accept the manuscript. They prepared for the release of the book in 1965 with special security precautions in case of outbreaks of violence at bookstores across the country.

The book was a resounding success. The *New York Times*, which had condemned Malcolm as "a twisted, ruthless, and vio-

The Black Panthers

Malcolm X's stance against white society and his message of black pride inspired other radical political movements. One of the groups that developed, in part because of Malcolm X, was the Black Panthers. The Panthers, according to journalist Jessica Christina Harris, "maintain that African-Americans can not achieve liberation in the United States within the existing political and economic system. Therefore, they call for revolution to rid the society of capitalism, imperialism, racism, and sexism." The Panthers found Malcolm's rhetoric too moderate for their tastes but agreed with him that blacks had a duty to retaliate against violent attacks.

The Black Panther movement was founded in the fall of 1966 by two young black militants, Huey P. Newton and Bobby Seale, both of Oakland, California. A third important member, Eldridge Cleaver, joined in the late 1960s after his release from prison. Together, the three blacks created a party dedicated to advancing the cause of black freedom by revolutionary means.

Their advocacy of violence and revolution appealed to thousands of young African Americans throughout the United States. In addition to their revolutionary rhetoric, the Black Panther Party worked for African Americans in the San Francisco area by providing free breakfasts to all the schoolchildren in the Bay Area.

Jessica Christina Harris, "Revolutionary Black Nationalism: The Black Panther Party," *Journal of Negro History*, June 22, 2000.

lent man," hailed the autobiography as a "brilliant, painful, important book."[82] *Time* magazine had also been extremely critical of Malcolm X but eventually listed the book as one of the ten best nonfiction books of the twentieth century.

Reviewers praised Malcolm's realism and his honest self-appraisal. One reviewer wrote: "Here one may read, in the agony of this brilliant Negro's self-esteem, the agony of an entire people in their search for identity."[83] Most other reviews were just as positive. The book sold well and offered readers an intimate look at the hard life Malcolm had lived.

Shortly after the book's release, producer Marvin Worth acquired the movie rights. Nearly twenty-five years would pass, however, before the book could be brought to the big screen. Worth struggled to find the right cast and director, as well as the financial support to make the movie. Eventually, the movie *Malcolm X* was released in 1992. African American director Spike Lee presented a very realistic look at Malcolm X's life. Actor Denzel Washington, who had portrayed Malcolm X on Broadway, was named to play the black leader in the film. Malcolm's widow, Betty Shabazz, served as a consultant for the film. The movie has been praised for its realism; it also helped rekindle Malcolm's message of racial justice and racial pride.

Malcolm Mania

The Autobiography of Malcolm X, along with the movie based on the book, were two factors in the growing popularity of Malcolm X. A *Newsweek* poll in the 1990s found that 82 percent of black Americans considered Malcolm a strong black male figure. In addition, legions of young whites also made him an icon. During his lifetime, Malcolm X was considered a radical, a hatemonger, and an advocate of violence; today he is praised as a heroic black nationalist who dared to say the things thousands of blacks were too afraid to speak of themselves.

Malcolm became such a popular cult figure that Shabazz had to file suit to protect the use of his name from crass commercialism. In spite of this, thousands of T-shirts bearing his name and image are worn by college students across the country. Cone explains: "Young Blacks love Malcolm almost to the point of uncritical adoration. . . . He expresses the anger they feel about White America and about the Black leadership establishment. That is why Malcolm is popular among rap artists and street preachers and why his image and sayings adorn buttons, caps, and t-shirts."[84]

To help preserve Malcolm's place in history, the Malcolm X and Dr. Betty Shabazz Memorial and Educational Center in New York City opened in May 2005, to mark what would have been Malcolm's eightieth birthday. The opening ceremonies were led by Malcolm and Betty's daughter Alyasah Shabazz. She stated: "I think when we put it all in perspective, what you cannot help but to appreciate and to admire [were] his integrity, his passion, and his . . . quest for justice and for freedom for all of us."[85] The center features hundreds of mementos from his life, including love letters

Actor Denzel Washington appears here in a scene from the movie *Malcolm X*, in which he portrayed the late African American leader.

Betty Shabazz

———◼———

Malcolm's wife, Betty, was left to raise four daughters on her own after his death. For the most part, Betty avoided publicity and opted, instead, to provide a quiet, stable home life and education for her children. While she made occasional appearances on behalf of civil rights, she preferred the role of mother and teacher.

She also began to further her own education as well. Between 1970 and 1975 she completed a master's degree in public health administration and received her doctorate in education from the University of Massachusetts at Amherst. She joined the faculty at Medgar Evers College in Brooklyn, New York, and eventually became one of the university's directors.

On June 1, 1997, Shabazz suffered third-degree burns over 80 percent of her body in a fire started by her grandson, Malcolm. During the next three weeks, Betty fought for her life and underwent five different operations to replace burned skin. She eventually succumbed to the injuries on June 23, 1997.

A memorial service attracted more than two thousand friends and supporters. Her friend Wilbert Tatum, the publisher of the *Amsterdam News*, spoke of her impact: "Betty had impact far beyond that which most of us realized. She taught us all the meaning of commitment, the understanding and acceptance of tragedy and then moving on."

Quoted in Dale Russakoff and Blaine Harden, "Betty Shabazz Dies of Burn Injuries," *Washington Post*, June 24, 1997.

Malcolm X's widow, Betty Shabazz, opted for privacy after her husband's death, preferring the role of mother and teacher to that of civil rights leader.

he wrote to his wife. Other exhibits include various photographs, the shell casings from the guns that killed him, and copies of his many speeches.

Legacy

Malcolm X was underappreciated during his lifetime; only since his death has he achieved praise and a positive place in American history. Goldman, for instance, says: "Malcolm . . . was a revolutionary of the spirit. . . . He said the things black people had been afraid to say, even to think, for all those years; he got it all out in the open, the secrets and the guilts and the hypocrisies that underlay the public mythology of the great melting pot."[86] The tragedy is that most of his message got lost in the scary and violent image he projected.

Friedly also views Malcolm in a positive light:

> Malcolm X's passionate rhetoric did not just benefit the black community. Malcolm was also the conscience of white society in America. He nagged them and cajoled them for their inhumane actions against African Americans. . . . Malcolm X refused to allow the African Americans to be forgotten. He was the uncompromising critic of white society who jolted many white listeners to the conclusion that he was right, that America's rigid racial hierarchy had to be abolished.[87]

Malcolm X was among the first black spokespersons to take issue with the word "Negro." In advocating the use of the words "black" and "African American," he helped generate black pride and also the inclusion of black study programs at universities throughout the country. *Chicago Tribune* writer Salim Muwakkil agrees: "With his emphasis on alternative scholarship, Malcolm is also cited as a progenitor of the Black Studies academic movement."[88] In addition, he influenced many African Americans to become interested in their African and Islamic roots. The number of blacks adopting Muslim names has dramatically increased in the last four decades.

Philadelphia Tribune reporter Greg Johnson praises Malcolm X because of this emphasis on black pride. He writes: "He restored dignity to the Black soul. For centuries, African Americans had

Malcolm X's legacy lives on, in part through the many books written about him.

been told they were nothing. Malcolm X gave pride to a dishonored race. He was their 'gallant young champion' who didn't hesitate to die because he loved them so."[89]

Author Bruce Perry concludes:

Malcolm X fathered no legislation. He engineered no stunning Supreme Court victories or political campaigns. . . . Yet, because of the way he articulated his followers' grievances and anger, the impact he had upon the body politic was enormous. He mobilized black America's dormant rage and put it to work politically. He made clear the price that white America would have to pay if it did not accede to black America's legitimate demands. . . . He irrevocably altered America's political landscape.[90]

Notes

Introduction: The Evolution of Malcolm X

1. Charles Whitaker, "Who Was Malcolm X?" *Ebony*, February 1, 1992.
2. Desair E. Brown, "Malcolm X: Father's Murder Led to Troubled Childhood," *Washington Afro-American*, June 28, 1997.
3. Quoted in Malcolm X with Alex Haley, *The Autobiography of Malcolm X*. New York: Grove, 1964, p. ix.
4. Peter Goldman, *The Death and Life of Malcolm X*. Urbana: University of Illinois Press, 1979, p. 221.
5. Quoted in Africa Within, "Malcolm X Quotes." www.africa within.com/malcolmx/quotes .htm.

Chapter One: A World of Violence and Segregation

6. Malcolm X with Haley, *The Autobiography of Malcolm X*, p. 3.
7. Colorado State University Muslim Student Association, "Malcolm X—an Islamic Perspective," www.colostate.edu/Orgs/MSA/ find_more/m_x.html.
8. Malcolm X with Haley, *The Autobiography of Malcolm X*, p. 10.

9. Malcolm X with Haley, *The Autobiography of Malcolm X*, p. 22.
10. Quoted in James H. Cone, *Martin and Malcolm and America: A Dream or a Nightmare*. Maryknoll, NY: Orbis, 1992, p. 44.
11. Malcolm X with Haley, *The Autobiography of Malcolm X*, p. 33.
12. Quoted in Bruce Perry, *Malcolm: The Life of a Man Who Changed Black America*. Barrytown, NY: Station Hill, 1991, p. 42.
13. Goldman, *The Death and Life of Malcolm X*, p. 29.

Chapter Two: "Detroit Red"

14. Malcolm X with Haley, *The Autobiography of Malcolm X*, p. 41.
15. Malcolm X with Haley, *The Autobiography of Malcolm X*, p. 43.
16. Michael Friedly, *Malcolm X: The Assassination*. New York: Carroll and Graf, 1992, p. 9.
17. Goldman, *The Death and Life of Malcolm X*, p. 30.
18. Malcolm X with Haley, *The Autobiography of Malcolm X*, p. 180.
19. Quoted in Robert James Branham, "'I Was Gone on Debating': Malcolm X's Prison Debates and Public Confrontations," *Argumentation and Advocacy*, January 1, 1995.

Chapter Three: Minister Malcolm X

20. Cone, *Martin and Malcolm and America*, p. 10.
21. Nation of Islam, "Nation of Islam in America." www.noi.org/history_of_noi.htm.
22. Malcolm X with Haley, *The Autobiography of Malcolm X,* p. 163.
23. *Time*, "Recruits Behind Bars," March 31, 1961. www.time.com/time/magazine/article/0,9171,872173,00.html.
24. Quoted in Cone, *Martin and Malcolm and America*, p. 163.
25. Malcolm X with Haley, *The Autobiography of Malcolm X*, p. 198.
26. Quoted in David Gallen, *Malcolm: A to X: The Man and His Ideas*. New York: Carroll and Graf, 1992, p. 11.
27. Keith A. Owens, "Black Rage, Black Power," *Michigan Chronicle*, February 28, 2006.
28. Malcolm X with Haley, *The Autobiography of Malcolm X*, p. 212.
29. Goldman, *The Death and Life of Malcolm X*, p. 12.
30. Quoted in Joe Wood, *Malcolm X in Our Own Image*. New York: St. Martin's, 1992, p. 48.
31. Quoted in Official Website of Malcolm X, "Quotes by Malcolm X." www.cmgww.com/historic/malcolm/about/quotes_by.htm.
32. Cone, *Martin and Malcolm and America*, p. 95.
33. Quoted in Cone, *Martin and Malcolm and America*, p. 181.
34. Cone, *Martin and Malcolm and America*, p. 95.
35. Cone, *Martin and Malcolm and America*, p. 100.
36. Sulayman Nyang, "The Evolution of the Man Known as Malcolm Little, Malcolm X, and El-Hajj Malik el-Shabazz," *Los Angeles Sentinel*, May 21, 2003.

Chapter Four: A New Name—a New Outlook

37. Quoted in Cone, *Martin and Malcolm and America*, p. 191.
38. Malcolm X with Haley, *The Autobiography of Malcolm X*, p. 305.
39. Goldman, *The Death and Life of Malcolm X*, p. 247.
40. Quoted in Colorado State University Muslim Student Association, "Malcolm X—an Islamic Perspective."
41. Quoted in Colorado State University Muslim Student Association, "Malcolm X—an Islamic Perspective."
42. Malcolm X with Haley, *The Autobiography of Malcolm X*, p. 344.
43. Quoted in Colorado State University Muslim Student Association, "Malcolm X—an Islamic Perspective."
44. Margaret Snyder, "Malcolm After Mecca," *Commonweal*, December 18, 1992.
45. Quoted in *Michigan Citizen*, "A Conversation with Malcolm X," February 27, 1999.

46. Quoted in Whitaker, "Who Was Malcolm X?"
47. Quoted in Colorado State University Muslim Student Association, "Malcolm X—an Islamic Perspective."
48. Malcolm X with Haley, *The Autobiography of Malcolm X*, p. 317.
49. Malcolm X, "Malcolm X's Speech at the Founding Rally of the Organization of Afro-American Unity," *Black Past*, June 28, 1964. www.blackpast.org/?q=1964-malcolm-x-s-speech-founding-rally-organization-afro-american-unity.
50. Quoted in Malcolm X, *By Any Means Necessary*. New York: Pathfinder, 1970, p. xv.
51. Quoted in Wood, *Malcolm X in Our Own Image*, p. 49.
52. Malcolm X with Haley, *The Autobiography of Malcolm X*, p. 278.
53. Quoted in *Militant*, "The Assassination of Malcolm X," vol. 59, no. 21, May 29, 1995.
54. Malcolm X, "After the Bombing Speech at Ford Auditorium," *Malcolm X Speeches*, February 14, 1965. www.malcolm-x.org/speeches/spc_021465.htm.
55. Malcolm X, "Malcolm X's Speech at the Founding Rally of the Organization of Afro-American Unity."
56. Quoted in William Dudley, ed.*The Civil Rights Movement: Opposing Viewpoints*. San Diego: Greenhaven, 1996, p. 107.
57. Malcolm X, *By Any Means Necessary*, p. 41.
58. Quoted in *Michigan Citizen*, "A Conversation with Malcolm X."
59. Quoted in Cone, *Martin and Malcolm and America*, p. 196.
60. Malcolm X with Haley, *The Autobiography of Malcolm X*, p. 373.
61. Malcolm X, "Malcolm X's Speech at the Founding Rally of the Organization of Afro-American Unity."
62. Quoted in Dudley, ed., *The Civil Rights Movement: Opposing Viewpoints*, p. 103.

Chapter Five: The Death and Legacy of Malcolm X

63. Karl Evanzz, "Deadly Crossroads: Farrakhan's Rise and Malcolm X's Fall," *Washington Post*, December 12, 1995.
64. Quoted in Evanzz, "Deadly Crossroads."
65. Malcolm X with Haley, *The Autobiography of Malcolm X*, p. 313.
66. Goldman, *The Death and Life of Malcolm X*, p. 3.
67. Quoted in Colorado State University Muslim Student Association, "Malcolm X—an Islamic Perspective."
68. Goldman, *The Death and Life of Malcolm X*, p. 4.
69. Quoted in Malcolm X with Haley, *The Autobiography of Malcolm X*, p. 434.
70. Friedly, *Malcolm X: The Assassination*, p. 10.
71. *Time*, "Death and Transfiguration," March 5, 1965. www.time

.com/time/magazine/article/0,917
1,839291,00.html.

72. Ossie Davis, "Malcolm X's Eulogy," Africa Within, February 27, 1965. www.africawithin.com/malcolmx/eulogy.htm.

73. Quoted in Friedly, *Malcolm X: The Assassination*, p. 10.

74. *Time*, "Death and Transfiguration."

75. Quoted in Evanzz, "Deadly Crossroads."

76. Quoted in Salim Muwakkil, "On Malcolm's 75th Birthday, Questions Remain About Assassination," Knight-Ridder/Tribune News Service, May 17, 2000.

77. Friedly, *Malcolm X: The Assassination*, p. 159.

78. Evanzz, "Deadly Crossroads."

79. Friedly, *Malcolm X: The Assassination*, p. 67.

80. Goldman, *The Death and Life of Malcolm X*, p. 38.

81. Cone, *Martin and Malcolm and America*, p. 208.

82. Quoted in Taylor Branch, *At Canaan's Edge: America in the King Years, 1965–1968*. New York: Simon and Schuster, 2006, p. 371.

83. Quoted in Branch, *At Canaan's Edge*, p. 374.

84. Quoted in Whitaker, "Who Was Malcolm X?"

85. Quoted in Farai Chideya, "Profile: Malcolm X and Dr. Betty Shabazz Memorial and Educational Center Opens," *NPR Special*, May 19, 2005.

86. Goldman, *The Death and Life of Malcolm X*, p. 399.

87. Friedly, *Malcolm X: The Assassination*, p. 27.

88. Muwakkil, "On Malcolm's 75th Birthday, Questions Remain."

89. Greg Johnson, "Malcolm X, King Were Not Enemies," *Philadelphia Tribune*, February 21, 2006.

90. Perry, *Malcolm X: The Life of a Man Who Changed Black America*, p. 380.

For More Information

Books

Michael Benson, *Malcolm X*. Minneapolis: Lerner, 2002. A comprehensive biography of Malcolm X.

David Collins, *Black Rage: Malcolm X*. New York: Dillon, 1992. A biography of Malcolm X.

Arthur Diamond, *Malcolm X: A Voice for Black America*. Hillside, NJ: Enslow, 1994. A biography of Malcolm X.

Laban Carrick Hill, *America Dreaming*. New York: Little, Brown, 2007. Describes the 1960s and the revolutionary changes that occurred from the viewpoint and actions of the youth of that time period.

Walter Dean Myers, *Malcolm X: By Any Means Necessary*. New York: Scholastic, 1993. A comprehensive biography of Malcolm X.

Jack Rummel, *Malcolm X: Militant Black Leader*. New York: Chelsea House, 1989. A comprehensive biography of Malcolm X.

Periodicals

Clayborne Carson, "Malcolm X, King: Could Twain Have Met?" *Washington Times*, February 11, 1998.

Arlene McKanic, "Why Malcolm X Left the Nation of Islam," *New York Amsterdam News*, August 25, 2004.

Luix Virgil Overbea, "Those Who Knew Malcolm X Share Impressions of His Life," *Bay State Banner*, October 28, 1993.

Abiola Sinclair, "Who Really Killed Malcolm X?" *New York Amsterdam News*, February 26, 1994.

Conrad W. Worrall, "The Legacy of Malcolm X," *Chicago Defender*, May 14, 2007.

Radio

Melissa Block, "Commentary: American Muslims Need Another Malcolm X," *All Things Considered*, NPR, February 21, 2005.

Internet Sources

AFRO, "Panthers 10 Point Program." www.afroam.org/history/Panthers/10point.html.

Malcolm X, "Malcolm X Speaks: It's the Ballot or the Bullet," *Malcolm X Speaks*, AfricaWithin.com. www.africawithin.com/malcolmx/malcolm_speaks.htm.

Malcolm X, "Program of the Organization of Afro-American Unity," MalcolmX.org. www.malcolm-x.org/docs/gen_oaau.htm.

Nation of Islam, "Minister Louis Farrakhan." www.noi.org/mlfbio.htm.

Official Website of Malcolm X,

"Quotes About Malcolm X."
www.cmgww.com/historic/
malcolm/about/quotes_about
.htm.

Time, "The Black Supremacists," August 10, 1959. www.time.com/
time/magazine/article/0,9171,8119
1.00.html.

———, "Conversion of the Muslims," March 14, 1977. www.time
.com/time/magazine/article/0,9171,
947278,00.html.

Web Sites

Brother Malcolm
(www.brothermalcolm.net). This
Web site offers a variety of information about Malcolm X,
including many of his speeches.

Official Website of Malcolm X
(www.cmgww.com/historic/mal
colm). This Web site offers a biography of the leader along with
other features, including many of
his speeches.

Index

A

Autobiography of Malcolm X (Malcolm X, Haley), 86–87

B

Bembry, John Elton, 35
Black Muslims. *See* Nation of Islam
Black nationalism, 6, 39, 40
Black Panther movement, 87
Black pride, 41, 71–72
Branham, Robert James, 37
Brown, Desair E., 6–7
Butler, Norman 3X, 81, 85

C

Civil rights movement
  FBI taps phones of leaders of, 75–76
  Malcolm changes views on, 7, 71, 72
  Malcolm condemns nonviolent approach of, 51–53
Clarke, Steve, 69
Cleaver, Eldridge, 87
Cone, James H., 39, 51, 58, 86

D

Davis, Ozzie, 81–83

Drew, Timothy, 40

E

Evans, Clara, 42
Evanzz, Karl, 76, 85

F

Fard, Wallace D., *40*, 40–41, 42, 44
Farrakhan, Louis, 76, *84*, 84–85
Federal Bureau of Investigation (FBI), 75–76
Friedly, Michael, 31–32, 80, 85, 91

G

Garvey Club, *16*
Garvey, Marcus, 13, *13*, 14, 40
Gill, Howard B., 37
Goldman, Peter, 9, 41, 49, 78, 91
Great Depression, 15

H

Haley, Alex, 7, 86
Harlem, 28, 30, 31, 51
  riots in, 30, *30*
Harris, Jessica Christina, 87
Hayer, Talmadge, 80–81, 84
Hinton, James, 53, 54

Hoover, J. Edgar, 75

J
Jarvis, Shorty, 25
Jim Crow laws, 11, *11*
Johnson, Greg, 91–92
Johnson, Thomas 15X, 81, 84

K
Kennedy, John F., 59
King, Coretta Scott, 71
King, Martin Luther, Jr., 7, 52, *52,
    70, 71*
Ku Klux Klan, 13
    attack on Little home by, 14–15

L
Lee, Spike, 88
Little, Earl (father), 10, 13–15
    killing of, 17
Little, Ella (half sister), 22, 23, 27
    home of (Boston, MA), 25
Little, Louise (mother), 10, 14–15,
    17, 19
Little, Malcolm. *See* Malcolm X

M
Malcolm X, *8, 65*
    arriving at firebombed home, 77
    assassination of, 79–81, *80*
    on blacks of Roxbury, MA, 24
    on blacks' right to self-defense,
        72
    on burning of Little home, 15
    at Charlestown Prison (MA), 34–37,
        36
    as child, 22
    comments on Kennedy
        assassination, 59, *60*
    conflict with hierarchy of Nation of
        Islam, 57–58
    on creation of Organization for
        Afro-American Unity, 68, *68*
    criminal life of, 31–35
    decision to speak about black
        grievances before United Nations,
        73–74, *74*
    develops interest in black history,
        35–37
    dodges World War II draft, 32
    early life of, 6–7, 10, 15, 17, 19–23,
        22
    with Elijah Muhammad, *47*
    on experience of the hajj, 64, 66
    on founding Organization of Afro-
        American Unity, 67–69, *68*
    funeral of, 81–83, *82*
    at Harlem rally, *50*
    with his children, *54*
    on killing of his father, 17
    legacy of, 91–92, *92*
    makes pilgrimage to Mecca, 62–64
    marries Sister Betty X, 54
    with Martin Luther King Jr., *70*
    media's condemnation of, 83
    meets with African leaders, 67
    mug shot of, *33*
    name change, meaning of, 46

at Norfolk Prison (MA), 37–38
with Prince Faisal al-Saud, *63*
studies Nation of Islam, 39–45
theories on assassination of,
  84–85
threats against, 76, 78
Malcolm X (film), 88
  Denzel Washington stars in, *89*
Marshall, Thurgood, 44–45
Mecca (Saudi Arabia), Malcolm's
  pilgrimage to, 7, 62–64, 66
Moorish Science Temple, 40
Muhammad, Elijah, 7, 42, *43, 47*
  on death of Malcolm, 83
  is charged with adultery, 58–59
  Malcolm's devotion to, 58
  Malcolm's first contacts with, 45,
  46
  views Malcolm as rival, 57
Muslim Mosque, Inc., 61
Muwakkil, Salim, 91

N
Nation of Islam, 39
  basic principles of, 41
  criticism of, 44–45
  founding of, 40–41
  growth under Malcolm X, 49
  Malcolm's conflict with hierarchy of,
  57–58
  Malcolm's final break with, 61
  television documentary on,
  55–56
National Association of Colored

People (NAACP), 49, 52
New York Times (newspaper), 83,
  86–87
Newton, Huey P., 87
Norfolk Prison (MA), *36, 37*
  debating program at, 37, 38
Nyang, Sulayman, 56

O
Organization of Afro-American Unity,
  67–69, 72
Owens, Keith A., 49

P
Parks, Rosa, 51
Perry, Bruce, 92
Poole, Elijah. *See* Muhammad,
  Elijah

S
al-Saud, Faisal (Saudi prince), *63, 67*
Seale, Bobby, 87
Segregation, 11
  in the North, 12
el-Shabazz, El-Hajj Malik, Malcolm
  takes name of, 66
Shabazz, Alyasah (daughter), 88
Shabazz, Betty (Sister Betty X, wife),
  54, 80, 88, 90, *90*
Shawarbi, Youssef, 62
Sister Betty X. *See* Shabazz, Betty
60 Minutes (TV program), 84
Small's Paradise, 28, *28–29*
Snyder, Margaret, 66

T

Tatum, Wilbert, 90

Time (magazine), 44, 81, 83, 87

U

Universal Negro Improvement
  Association, 13, 14, 15

W

Wallace, Mike, 55, *55*

Washington, Denzell, 88,
  89

West, Cornell, 49, 69

Whitaker, Charles, 6

Worth, Marvin, 87

Picture Credits

Cover photo: Michael Ochs Archives/Getty Images
AP Images, 25, 36, 40, 43, 47, 50, 65, 70
© Bettmann/Corbis, 18, 21, 28–29, 33, 74, 77, 80, 82
© Bureau L.A. Collection/Corbis, 89
© Jacques M. Chenet/Corbis, 92
© Corbis, 16
Manny Deneta/Getty Images, 84
Robert L. Haggins/Time Life Pictures/Getty Images, 54
© Rick Maiman/Sygma/Corbis, 90
Malcolm: The Life of a Man Who Changed Black America, Bruce Perry, Station
    Hill Press, 1992, 22
Francis Miller/Time Life Pictures/Getty Images, 52
© Jack Moebes/Corbis, 11
Robert Parent/Hulton Archive/Getty Images, 8
Robert Parent/Time Life Pictures/Getty Images, 60, 68
Pictorial Parade/Getty Images, 63
© Underwood and Underwood/Corbis, 13
© UPI/Corbis-Bettmann, 30

About the Author

Anne Wallace Sharp is the author of the adult book *Gifts*, a compilation of stories about hospice patients and their caregivers, and several children's books, including *Daring Pirate Women*. She has also written numerous magazine articles for both adults and juveniles. A retired registered nurse, Sharp has a degree in history. Her interests include reading, traveling, and spending time with her grandchildren, Jacob and Nicole. Sharp lives in Beavercreek, Ohio.